Be a Good Neighbor,
and Leave Me Alone.©

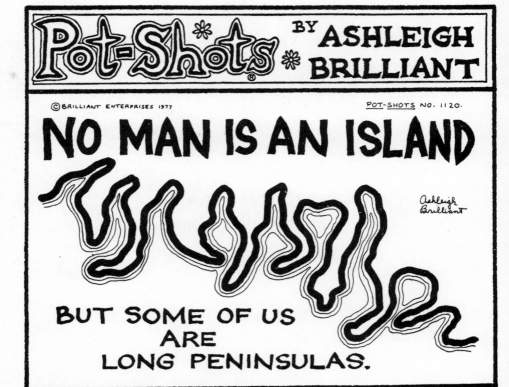

Pot-Shots BY ASHLEIGH BRILLIANT

© BRILLIANT ENTERPRISES 1977

POT-SHOTS NO. 1120.

NO MAN IS AN ISLAND

Ashleigh Brilliant

BUT SOME OF US
ARE
LONG PENINSULAS.

Be a Good Neighbor, and Leave Me Alone.©

... and Other Wry and Riotous Writings.

by

Ashleigh Brilliant

Creator of *Pot-Shots*,®
author of the Brilliant Thoughts® book series,
including, *I May Not Be Totally Perfect,
but Parts of Me Are Excellent,*© and other works.

Woodbridge Press Santa Barbara, California 93160

Published by

Woodbridge Press Publishing Company
Post Office Box 6189
Santa Barbara, California 93160

Copyright © 1992 by Ashleigh Brilliant

Distributed simultaneously in the United States and Canada.

Printed in the United States of America

Some of the essays in this collection first appeared
in *Santa Barbara Currents* and the *Santa Barbara Independent.*

Cover illustration by *Janice Blair.*

Library of Congress Cataloging-in-Publication Data:

Brilliant, Ashleigh, 1933-
Be a good neighbor, and leave me alone: and other wry and riotous
writings / by Ashleigh Brilliant.
p.   cm.
ISBN 0-88007-191-5 : $24.95. — ISBN 0-88007-192-3 (pbk.) : $12.95
1. Essays, American. 2. Satire. 3. Humor. I. Title.
PN6281.B663   1992
814'.54—dc20   91-26655
                                                         CIP

To the memory of GAGA (1975? - 1990)
Truly the World's Best Cat.

Table of Contents

●

Introduction

Look out! Here I come again, with another amazing act—but this time in a different costume. If you caught any of my previous literary performances, you have seen me mainly as a sparkling epigrammatist (in seven books of *Brilliant Thoughts,*® *1979-1990*), or as a sober (or at least semi-sober) social historian *(The Great Car Craze, 1989)*. Now I am asking you once more to suspend disbelief, and accept me as an essayist and as something of a poet.

That effort will probably be somewhat easier for you if by chance you have never heard of me, or of Pot-Shots,® before. Otherwise, I won't be at all surprised if, no matter what else I ever do, you insist on thinking of me primarily as the creator of those striking little cartoon-type messages, a few of which (for your sake) have been included in this book, but only as a sort of decoration. After all, it's not unusual for an author's lightest works to pigeonhole him forever in the public mind, regardless of anything else he may wish to be known for. Just ask that distinguished mathematician, Lewis Carroll, that gifted landscape painter, Edward Lear, or that great composer of hymns and oratorios, Sir Arthur Sullivan.

But if indeed Ashleigh Brilliant—yes, my real name—is new to you, I feel I should introduce myself, even though you will find various fragments of autobiographical data scattered herein. I am, at this writing, 57 years old, and have been living in Santa Barbara, California, since 1973. I was born in England, and my formal education included

extensive stretches on both sides of the Atlantic, cul-
minating with a Ph.D. in History at Berkeley in 1964.

After a few years of teaching (including two round-
the-world voyages with a Floating University) and a hippie
interlude in San Francisco, I stumbled into the unusual
career of marketing my own thoughts in the form of
illustrated epigrams, limited by my own rules to a
maximum of seventeen words. For about two decades, this
strange vocation largely absorbed my creative energies, but
eventually I began to feel confined by it, and started
writing essay-type pieces for publication in our local press.
It is a selection of these which forms the bulk of what you
will be reading in this book.

In addition, however, I have seized this opportunity to
lay before you three other kinds of offerings: 1. Miscellane-
ous short pieces of prose and poetry, rescued from diverse
crannies of my past life, which I have always liked, but
until now had no way of placing in your hands; 2. A few
self-indulgent pieces of personal reminiscense (my "War
Memoirs," "Going Down in History," "Faith, Soap, and
Charity," "Me and the Famous," and "I Go Bananas"), all
written specially for this volume; 3. A whole hodgepodge
of original jokes, ideas, and observations which have been
cluttering my mind and my files for many years.

The general principal of arrangement has been to
intermix these various types of material and distribute them
evenly throughout the book, thereby (and characteristically)
avoiding the task of imposing any more meaningful order
upon my life, and at least minimizing my risk of exceeding
your notoriously sensitive threshold of boredom.

Of course, I am hoping you will find more than mere
entertainment between these covers. Somebody recently
wrote to me that coming across one of my books
unexpectedly, after having lost touch with them for some
time, was like meeting an old friend. That must be one of
the kindest things anybody could say to an author (other
than in the form of cash or merchandise), and it has
inspired me to think of this book as an attempt to deepen
our friendship by giving you a little more of me to fasten

your own thoughts upon than has so far been available. But you have to play your part, too. The title affixed to this collection may sound somewhat unsociable, but don't let that deter you. Since you are (in all likelihood) not my neighbor, it should be much less difficult for you to become and remain my friend.

Santa Barbara 1991

© BRILLIANT ENTERPRISES 1975.

POT- SHOTS NO. 843.

It's possible that my whole purpose in life is simply to serve as a warning to others.

Ashleigh Brilliant

Ashleigh
Brilliant

INFORM ALL
THE TROOPS THAT
COMMUNICATIONS
HAVE
COMPLETELY
BROKEN
DOWN.

The Lost Cord

You never catch up—not any more. Maybe there was once a time when everything a person owned could be at the cutting edge of technology, in that totally trendy realm known as the State Of The Art. But today, there is simply too much happening too fast. I knew when I bought it that my new telephone was not really "new" at all—that other models on the market could perform far more elaborate tricks. But at least it had one feature which I had never before had at my command, one the very mention of which seems somehow to imply the ultimate in modernity—it was cordless!

Scholars have recently been convening to seek a metaphor for our age, some neat little verbal package to encapsulate the world as we know it, and set it off from all previous eras. If I may be permitted to join the game, I would designate ours as *The Age of Cordlessness.*

It begins, of course, in the womb—or rather, that is where it no longer needs to begin. With such miracles as *in vitro* fertilization and other feats of genetic engineering, our age is in the process of cutting its own umbilical cord. The generation which can still remember "Life With Father" may yet live to see the era of Birth Without Mother. For better or worse, we are learning to cut the apron strings before they have even been properly tied.

I pick up my cordless telephone to make my first call, which is naturally to my own mother, in Los Angeles. Following the instructions in the manual, I press a button marked PHONE. A little red light comes on, and, for some unaccountable reason, the device beeps at me. (Is this the Age of Beeps?) Then I hear a comfortingly familiar sound—the dial tone: that universal OM mantra which emanates from telephones all over the world. Within a few moments, another familiar sound reaches me from a hundred miles away: my mother's voice. And it's just as if that old cord were still there—the cord which has been so much a part of my life all these years, but to which I hardly ever gave even a passing thought, until it was gone.

Actually, for most of that time it was not one cord, but two. One of these, which could be very long if you paid the Telephone Company an extra charge, went from the main "base" part of the instrument (on which you dialed and "hung up"), through the wall of your house, to the Outer World. The other cord connected that "base" part with what was called the "handset"—the part you listened to and talked into. This second cord was, for some reason, always quite short, so that, no matter how long a main cord you had, you could never use the telephone without being more or less tied to that heavy base part, like a ball and chain. In old movies, you can still see agitated telephone users pacing about, pressing the handset to their head with one hand, while the base part, trailing its long cord, hangs from the fingers of their other hand.

Then all that changed. Possibly even within the memory of some teenagers now living, telephones suddenly became much smaller and lighter, and everything that used to be in two separate parts was incorporated into one simple hand-piece. Very liberating, but you were still stuck with a *cord*. This was the cord which, in our house, was always there to be tripped over (especially by unwary guests), to gather dust-balls and clumps of cat-hair in its coils, and to become, in the course of time, so hopelessly twisted that the only remedy was occasionally to stand on a chair dangling the device by its cord, and letting gravity, torque, and centrifugal force do the unwinding.

And now it is gone. And now (although the need has

never yet arisen), I can make a telephone call while running around the block, or from the roof of my house. ... And now also, not without a certain sadness, I begin to see that we are losing all our cords. Our toys and tellies now perform their functions under our cordless "remote control." Electric shavers and "dust-buster" vacuum-cleaners rejoice in their own cordlessness. Soon, no doubt, our live pets will no longer require the leashes or reins which once attached them to us, and us to them, but respond infallibly to the electronic commands of a little box.

How can we keep singing "Blest Be the Tie That Binds" as we approach what seems the inevitable time when everything will no longer need to be tangibly bound or connected to anything else? The roads and rails, the waterways and wire-ways, which once symbolized the binding-together of human life on this planet, are now more and more giving place to the "wire-less" and invisible "channels" of air and space. Divers and astronauts are shedding what used to be considered their "life-lines." The whole Universe, Science calmly informs us, is flying apart.

That inconvenient telephone cord may have meant more than we realized at the time. From the unsettling perspective of this strange new cordless world, my imagination begins to wonder if it did not represent the last string for finding our way back out of the forest. But time and technology have eaten it up, like the birds that ate Hansel's trail of crumbs. Yet, even though we can't go home again, the miracle is that I can somehow still hear my mother's voice.

Santa Barbara 1989

POT-SHOTS NO. 3578.

Ashleigh Brilliant

IS THERE LIFE

IN OTHER
FAMILIES?

Be a Good Neighbor, and Leave Me Alone.

Despite all pious injunctions to the contrary, something there is that doesn't love a neighbor. Neighbors are noisy when we want peace. Neighbors are grouchy when we want to make noise. Neighbors are curious when we want privacy, and unaware when we want to be noticed. Neighbors do things we don't like, and don't like things we do. Neighbors move in with no invitation from us, and move out just when we are getting used to them.

Neighbors probably have no idea how much they bother us with their cars, their kids, their animals, even with their trees and shrubbery. They live in their own neighbor-world, go to jobs, schools, shops, meetings, parties, countries, where only neighbors go. They know pathetically little about our lives, our interests, our sorrows.

Of course there are exceptions. I have even heard of people who married the girl next door. But it has never happened to me. In fact, my neighbors never even consult me about whom they do marry. And if or when they divorce, sometimes I am the last to be told.

We all know—at least we've been told often enough—what friends are for. But what are neighbors for? They roll up one day with their big moving-van, and suddenly a house which may have been innocently empty for months becomes full of them. And by the mere accident of proximity they automatically acquire that magic status of

19

"neighbor," which is supposed to entitle them to so much of our regard and concern.

So then begins the charade of welcoming them to our vicinity, introducing ourselves, making symbolic gifts, offering help, imparting the gossip and folklore which constitute the cultural heritage of our "neighborhood." What happens after that? Usually nothing. They don't need our help. They don't need *us*, any more than we ever needed them.

Things weren't always like this of course—not even in Santa Barbara where I live. In the days before telephones and automobiles, there was much more reason to be neighborly with your neighbors. In those distant times, the expression "since we're neighbors, let's be friends" had a compelling meaning. Now, significantly, it has been appropriated and debased as the slogan of a supermarket chain, and nothing short of a fire, accident, or natural disaster brings neighbors truly together.

But neighborliness has never been the whole story, especially in this country, which was largely built by people getting away from their neighbors. Our folk heroes, whatever their other virtues, were never famous for being neighborly. In frontier days, when you could hear the sound of your neighbor's dog, that's when it was time to "pull up stakes and head for the tall timber."

If we were a truly neighborly society, how could the love of firearms ever have seized such a mad grip upon our national consciousness? Does Superman or Batman have neighbors? Does any big celebrity have neighbors? Of course not. The very idea is absurd. As soon as we could afford to do so, most of us, you can bet, would move to some situation where we would no longer have to deal with people whose only real claim upon us is that they just happen to live near us. Money may not be able to buy happiness, but one thing it *can* buy is *space*.

Can you think of a folk song that even mentions neighbors? Can you think of a book or movie that treats the theme of neighbors in a positive way? Only from the pulpit are neighbors extolled, yet when ministers hit the headlines it is often because they themselves may have loved their neighbor a little too literally.

Since some of my own neighbors will no doubt be reading this, I must naturally claim that (fortunately for me) nothing herein applies to them. Even less, of course, does it apply to me myself in my own charming role as a neighbor to them. Still I hope we may all admit to finding something more than a jolly chuckle in the story of the child who recited:

"And on the seventh day, God rested from his neighbors."

Santa Barbara 1990

Pot-Shots ® BY ASHLEIGH BRILLIANT

© ASHLEIGH BRILLIANT 1983.

POT-SHOTS NO. 2875.

Ashleigh Brilliant

WHY SHOULD I LET YOU
INTO MY PRIVATE HELL?

Sanctuary Much

Safe places are naturally very much in demand in an unsafe world. The old religious idea was that God was the ultimate protector, and that, no matter what you had done, if you could get inside a church, your enemies would not dare to harm you there. Since your enemies usually believed the same thing, the system often worked. This charming notion has, however, now gone the way of trial by ordeal, human and animal sacrifice, and many other quaint old customs.

But the idea of sanctuary still has great appeal. Today the same kind of service is sometimes provided by embassies, where at least certain kinds of fugitives, if they are lucky, may be protected by the Gods of Diplomacy. But it is of course far preferable, if you can, to get out of the country altogether. This involves crossing that romantic line known as a border or frontier. "If only we can get across the border, we'll be safe" has been a theme of countless movies.

Strange as it seems in our "global village," those magic lines where something may be illegal on one side and quite kosher on the other still exist all over the world. For example, it always astonishes me that at a certain point as you cross the great American desert, that which is considered the crime and sin of gambling in most other places suddenly becomes open and respectable. What makes it even more bizarre is that the border in question is not even international, but only a line between federated

23

states. The desert is there on both sides, but only on one side of the line does the one-armed bandit receive this blessed (or cursed) protection.

Actually, the most common of all these "safety zones" (if you don't count the ultimate one inside your own cranium) is the "property line." "A man's home is his castle." There are of course certain things you are not supposed to do even at home. But what I like to call the Rite of Privacy offers a certain degree of magical security.

In many countries it is the universities which provide safe havens, and their campuses are generally considered to be off-limits to police and troops. Even there, however, for a person like me, other forms of menace can be much harder to avoid. I spent most of the years from 1952 to 1964 as a student at various universities, and wrote the following when at Berkeley in 1963:

Do Not Disturb

I had a book which I wanted to read, and I wanted to read it undisturbed. Outside, it was a beautiful day to sit and read, but there were people milling about everywhere, talking, shouting, laughing—so I went into the Library. But the reading room, too, was full of people. Pretty girls distracted me. Some people were whispering, others coughing or sniffling.

So I retreated up into the stacks. But still there was no getting away from people. As I sat at an open table, graduate students and library workers moved up and down the aisles, making disturbing noises. I was forced to take refuge in my little cubicle, walled in with steel partitions on three and one half sides. Yet even here people went back and forth by the opening, and there was no way I could close them out. One of them even said Hello to me.

Finally in desperation I went into the little stack-toilet, locked the door, and resolved that I would not open it for anyone. At last I was able to sit down in peace, on the toilet seat, and start reading my book, How to Get Along with People.

Wit's My Line

I am constantly getting funny ideas, but have never used most of them because they don't fit into the POT-SHOTS format, and until now I have had no other outlet for them. What a relief, then, to be able to inflict upon you the following dainty assortment. (Bore me if I stop you.)

❖ I'd advise you, Cyrano, to keep a low profile.

❖ Cleopatra's swan-song: "Fangs for the Mammary."

❖ There's nothing like a Notre Dame.

❖ Why is he called the CO-PILOT?
—Because he has to COPE with the PILOT.

❖ Sammy Davis Jr. is the one eye love.

❖ If I order a psychiatrist by mail,
will he arrive SHRINK-WRAPPED?

❖ Where does R2D2 do his Christmas shopping?
—At Sears Robot.

❖ We're off in our motor-home
for a weekend in the great indoors.

❖ Poor fellow—his computer developed a tumor.

❖ How long may it take the Swiss to win independence?
—Only time WILL TELL.

❖ Should Vatican Radio be called the Station of the Cross?

❖ WHAT'S THE NAME OF GOD?
Doesn't everybody know: "HAROLD be thy name."

❖ When the Italian made two bad marriages at the same time, it was a BIGAMISTAKE.

❖ Lusting is disgusting,
but too much virtue can hirtue.

❖ I didn't mind being a public executioner,
once I got the hang of it.

❖ With Bed and Breakfast now so popular, how about:
Sofa and Supper?
Lounge and Lunch?
Settee and Snack?

❖ I just wasn't cut out to be a paper doll.

❖ You know it's time to diet when your wedding-ring disappears somewhere inside your finger.

❖ Proposed New Magazines:
PENDULUM—the Magazine for Swingers.
KILL—takes you where the violence is.
THE NEW PORKER—for the modern piggery.
THEM—the Magazine for Paranoids.
RESTROOM NEWS—the Traveller's Best Friend.

❖ Matricide's Memoirs: I DISMEMBER MAMA.

❖ COUGH YOUR WAY TO HEALTH
Classes now forming—learn effective coughing techniques.

❖ SHOOT-OUT AT THE BACH CHORALE
With Doc Holiday, Wyatt Christmas Earp,
and the Well-Tempered Reindeer.

❖ THIS MONSTROUS PRACTICE MUST CEASE!
Join the movement to ban the extraction of Baby Oil from babies.

❖ He put it towards his Pension Fund: He had a penchant for blondes.

❖ She became a lawyer, and lost her appeal.

❖ That great song about NINE EYES:
NINE EYES have seen the glory of the coming of the Lord.

❖ The Dickens masterpiece which sweeps the reader from the seamy alleys of Hong Kong to the suave salons of Savile Row: A TAILOR OF TWO CITIES

❖ A STITCH IN TIME—will never repair your wrist-watch.

❖ A BIRD IN THE HAND—can be messy and uncomfortable.

❖ Introducing her wealthy husband-to-be: "This is my finance."

❖ We approached the bridge, resolved to give no quarter, but the merciless guards took their toll.

❖ They're called Generic products because they come from Generia.

❖ Clapper?...Clapper?... Yes, the name does ring a bell.

❖ When asked how his food supplies were holding out, he said he was just beginning to PEEL THE FINCH.

❖ Robin Hoodwink, the new-style mugger, forces people to take money at gunpoint.

❖ Why are they called waiters, when what they do is keep other people waiting?

❖ Where do all the TV scriptwriters live? —In Sitcom Valley.

❖ When the cows come home, I hope they bring good moos.

POT- SHOTS NO. 2607.

THE FUNNIEST THINGS

ARE SAID AND DONE

BY PEOPLE
WHO
ARE NOT
TRYING
TO BE
FUNNY.

Ashleigh Brilliant

Funny
You Should Say That

I have always enjoyed unintentional humor—even when the laugh is on myself. Once at school in England, we were having a class discussion about theater admission prices, and I said, "I object to the tax on the seats." There was a pause, and somebody said, "Then why don't you take them off?" It took some time for me to realize why everybody was laughing.

The longest and loudest laugh I ever remember hearing at that school (or any other) came when a very prim female art teacher was explaining to our drawing class how clothing follows the contours of the body. When drawing a clothed woman, she said quite innocently, "You've got to *FEEL* the leg beneath the skirt."

For devotees of this sort of thing, one especially hallowed location is the back pages of the *New Yorker* magazine, with their often exquisite "fillers," culled from a wide variety of sources. Considering the prestige of getting into the *New Yorker* under any pretext, I am proud of having succeeded, just once, in sending in an item which they used. It was extracted from a report I had seen in a London newspaper concerning a "pirate" radio station which was broadcasting to England from a ship moored offshore. It stated that the mailing address of the station, as given on the air, was a post office box at "Graham Central Station, New York." Who could possibly make such a mistake? Only some very unsophisticated British reporter in a land where "grand"

and "graham" are pronounced very similarly. I thought this might tickle the urbane *New Yorker* editors, and was myself quite tickled when it did. (Unfortunately, they are so urbane that they don't even credit their filler-contributors—but I did get $10 for it.)

In recent years, I have made a practice of writing down any particularly striking or outrageous "howlers" which I happen to hear on radio or TV (together with particulars of the program, lest anyone accuse me of fabricating these gems). Sometimes they are just slips of the tongue, in which people cross a body of water in a "Hoovercraft," or the President gets chosen by an "Electrical College." I am particularly charmed by spoonerisms. I once heard an announcer refer to the disease of "kidner cancy." Another reported on a meeting of "shock and stairholders." And I heard Jimmie Carter characterized as "a relatively leak weeder."

Sometimes the humor comes from what I *thought* I heard. For example, I could have sworn I heard the news reporter say, "The Prince changed a tire for an afternoon wreath-laying ceremony." This conjured up a very odd image in my mind, and it was only after some minutes of puzzlement that I realized that the Prince must really have "changed attire"!

Then there are just those very odd ways of expressing things:

"Melosovich overstepped his hand."

"We are reluctant to cast a suspicious finger at a parent."

"You know, it's hard for some of us to fathom that kind of flooding."

"... people on the lower end of the economic rung..."

"... AIDS is the new kid on the overall disease block."

"Ghadafi, like a jilted lover, ordered his men home."

For some reason, it is with the use of violent imagery that speakers seem particularly liable to get into trouble, and I have heard such pronouncements as these:

"It's not the end of this process by a long shot"—(Secretary of State Schultz, on the nuclear arms negotiations).

"The battlefield performance of the Contras is under fire."

"Schevernadze charged that the U.S. has poisoned the atmosphere of this week's chemical weapons conference."

"The Defense Secretary seemed defensive to me."

"The President stuck to his guns on a space-based missile system."

"More than a dozen local groups are shooting for a fatality-free weekend."

One of my most treasured exhibits came out of a news report I heard on August 9, 1986, concerning President Reagan's urological problems, in which it was stated that "the President passed a milestone today."

Another of my prize specimens is this: "We became concerned about four years ago with improving the condition of the trails. They were going downhill due to lack of funds from the Federal Government."

But the showpiece of my entire collection was captured on November 2, 1988. On a Public Radio report about animal rights activists, it was alleged that such people were just a small group of fanatical vegetarians. To this I swear I heard their spokesman reply: "That's hog-wash. This is a real grass roots movement."

Santa Barbara 1990

POT-SHOTS NO. 1523

I WANT ETERNAL LIFE,

OR SOMETHING JUST AS GOOD.

© ASHLEIGH BRILLIANT 1979

Ashleigh Brilliant

A Little Gift
of Immortality

A: I wish I didn't have to die. Life seems so meaningless if we all have to die.

B: Very well, then, I hereby grant you immortality.

A: Really? You mean I can stop worrying about aging and dying?

B: That's just what I mean.

A: I'll just go on living for ever and ever, without changing?

B: Not exactly. You'll still change, but you just won't die. You wouldn't want never to change at all, would you?

A: I guess not, since everything I do changes me in some way, and so does everything that happens to me.

B: Then you'll change and wear out, but, as you do, your parts will be replaced.

A: Even my brain?

B: Yes.

A: How will I know that I'm still me?

B: The same way you know now, even though you're very different from the baby you once were.

A: But will I remember everything?

B: You don't remember everything now. You'll remember some things, and forget others.

A: And this will go on and on forever?

B: Yes, forever.

A: What about my family and friends?

B: It will be just the same with them. You will all be immortal forever.

A: What about all the people who are already dead?
B: For them, unfortunately, it's too late.

A: What will we do with all our time?
B: The same things you do now, if you wish.

A: But so many of them will seem rather meaningless now, if we're all going to live forever. There'll be no need to take care of ourselves or each other, no need to reproduce, no need, really, to do anything, because there will always be more time to do it later.
B: Pardon me, but weren't you just complaining that it was death that made life meaningless? Isn't that why I gave you immortality?

A: I want immortality on my own terms.
B: Which are —?

A: Meaningful immortality. Enough going on forever in the world to provide continuity and permanence. Enough changing and ending to give dimension and substance.
B: But that is what you have always had.

On a Greyhound bus, January 16, 1979

On a Roll

The TV commercial was very simple, but it made me gasp, and it practically made my wife fall out of her chair. All it showed, besides the product being advertised, was a roll of toilet paper, with some sub-titled days of the week. On the first three days, the roll is hanging idly on its roller. On the final day, it is being unrolled, as if in actual use, by unseen hands. The commercial is not for toilet paper, but for a laxative, and the message is clear and effective.

Why were we so surprised? Because we could hardly recall ever before having seen an *unwrapped* roll of toilet paper depicted on television in any connection, and certainly never with any suggestion of its true role in our lives. And, no matter how much sex and violence the American public is prepared to tolerate in the media, we had always assumed that what takes place in what is itself euphemistically known as the "bathroom" was sacrosanct.

We were accustomed to seeing toilet paper (always discreetly referred to as "bathroom tissue"), appearing, if at all, always in its charming wrapper, in advertisements featuring innocent bow-tied druggists and doe-eyed children, whispering of "softness" and "squeezability." Laxative commercials, in order to avoid all risk of offending, have traditionally not only kept out of the bathroom, but stayed out of the home altogether, instead depicting happy users enjoying their freedom from constipation in some outdoor sporting activity, or pleasantly busy at their places of employment. (I have to be careful with a subject like this—I nearly said "on the job.")

Now suddenly we are confronted—and in prime time—with the amazing suggestion that there is some connection between the use of laxatives and the use of toilet paper. Compared with such a startling development, the fall of the Berlin Wall is but a minor incident. And indeed one wonders whether both events may not be part of a great wave of openness, perhaps still in its early stages, which is sweeping the world. In the heady delirium of winning the Cold War, we may now stand in danger of seeing our cherished ideals of anal prudery overwhelmed by an avalanche of European earthiness.

The only way to deal with this menace may be to ignore all promises of "regularity" and refuse to use any such product whose advertising is at all irregular. It sounds like the beginning of a great new consumer movement.

(Oops! Sorry.)

Santa Barbara 1990

Bits and Pieces

Hostess with the Mostest

My cat is free of all disease—
That is, if I don't count fleas—
But fleas she has in such amount
I really haven't time to count!

January 1987

Way to Go

I have decided how I want to die. I want to be killed in the manner of Aeschylus, by having a tortoise accidentally dropped on my head by a passing eagle. Death should of course be instantaneous for me—but I hope the tortoise survives, and the eagle finds another meal.

August 1988

Cold Comfort

Life is real!
Life is earnest!
Go, my dear,
And stoke the furnace.

1985

The Theology of Peanut Butter

Ever since I became a wise man, people have been interested in the beliefs which underlie my wisdom. As is by now well-known, my own personal faith is founded upon a belief in peanut butter. If there remain any uncertainties concerning this, the following dialog should clear them up:

Q: When you say you believe in peanut butter, does that mean that God is peanut butter?
A: On the contrary, it means that peanut butter is God.

Q: Why do you believe in peanut butter?
A: Because it is perfectly reliable and perfectly benevolent.

Q: Does it matter if the peanut butter is smooth or chunky?
A: I personally believe in smooth peanut butter. But I try to be tolerant. Some of my best friends believe in the chunky kind.

Q: What ethical code can be derived from your belief?
A: Treat all beings as if you were totally dependent upon them for your next peanut butter experience.

Q: Have peanut butter believers any holy places?
A: Somewhere in Tibet there is said to be a whole mountain of peanut butter, but no pilgrim who has gone in search of it has ever returned. To the ordinary believer, every jar is a shrine.

Q: What form of prayer or hymn do you find appropriate?
A: The truly devout believer will always substitute the words "Peanut Butter!" for "Hallelujah!" in the "Hallelujah Chorus."

Q: Do you believe in an after-life?
A: The question is absurd. How can there be a life after peanut butter?

Q: If peanut butter is the greatest good, is its absence the greatest evil?
A: No. There is one much greater evil.

Q. And what is that?
A: Loose dental plates.

San Francisco, July 1967

The
Seven Second Delay

It always used to bother me to know that the supposedly "live" radio program I was hearing was actually being recorded, and then broadcast seven seconds later. Of course, I knew why they were doing it. Usually the program was some kind of call-in show, and the delay gave the host time to prevent anything too outrageous that might be said from going out on the air. Even so, it didn't seem right to deprive us listeners of the truly live instantaneous communication which radio makes possible.

With this kind of impatience, you can imagine how hard I have always found it to comprehend what life must have been like in times past, when it often took months, or even years, to get word from one place on this planet to another. Wouldn't it have been terribly frustrating, for example, to be living in California early in the last century, and not get news even of world-shaking events like the Battle of Waterloo until something like a year after they had happened? How on Earth did people correspond meaningfully with one another when the letter just received from your distant brother might report that he's in perfect health, whereas in fact (as you will learn sometime next year) he has just died after a long illness?

Even in more recent times, keeping in touch has not always been easy. Ernest Shackleton tells in his great book,

South, how he left England on an expedition to Antarctica in 1914, just after the outbreak of a war which was expected to be over before Christmas. Two years later, when he first re-established contact with civilization, staggering into a whaling station on South Georgia island, one of the first questions he asked was, "When was the war over?" He was amazed to be told, "It's not over! It's still going on! Millions are being killed! Europe is mad! The world is mad!"

But even today, if you turn your attention from this mad world to the wider world of the Cosmos, the communication picture is hardly more consoling. The speed of light may be the fastest thing in the Universe, but it is still so painfully slow that the information it brings us can be thousands or millions of years out of date.

None of this, however, is going to worry me any more—not since I figured out the perfect answer to the problem of the seven second delay. It involves one of those "thought experiments" of the kind that Einstein made so popular—the only one I myself have ever devised. Let's imagine that, instead of broadcasting on the radio, the speaker, wherever he is, can shout loud enough, with his own unaided voice, for me to hear him where I am. The speaker who normally hosts one of my favorite radio shows happens to be in Los Angeles, and I happen to be in Santa Barbara—a distance of about 100 miles. Since the speed of sound is only a sluggish 764 miles an hour, this means that his words would not reach me for about *eight minutes!* So even with the seven-second delay, I'm actually getting him by radio much more "immediately" than if I were hearing him live and direct. On that evidence, I've decided to spare his vocal cords, and settle for the slight delay. After all, it's good to know those seven seconds are helping to keep the air sanitized for my protection.

Santa Barbara 1990

Cynosure

Many of them were already there by the time I arrived. They were busy setting up easels and work-stands, arranging tools and paints and clay—a mixed group of housewives, business-men, and students, all gathered for an evening of creative relaxation. It was quite a small studio, and they all stood chatting together within a few feet of the empty platform

Summoning up my courage, I walked over to Vito who, as usual, was bandying loud wisecracks with one of the group.

"Well....here I am!" I stammered.

"Ah, so you made it. Well, good!" and he returned to his conversation.

"But....but, what do I do now?" I asked, struggling to regain his attention.

"Get undressed, of course. You can use the room upstairs. ... Look son, I know this is your first time, but there's really nothing to worry about. We're not interested in *you*. It's just your body we're concerned with. Now hurry up. It's almost time to start. And remember, no shorts or straps. Get right in the raw."

Moving slowly upstairs, I looked down on the platform surrounded by men and women and wondered if two dollars an hour was worth an ordeal like this, even if I did have to pay the rent tomorrow. I felt glad that I had at least brought a dressing-gown, so that I would not have to make that long stairway descent in the nude.

41

When they were at last ready to begin, Vito motioned to me, where I had been sitting in a corner in my dressing-gown, trying to look inconspicuous. "Now or never," I said to myself, and, with a quick motion, flung off the gown, and stepped boldly onto the platform.

For some reason, I had expected an awed hush to descend upon the group—but the chatter went on as before. In fact, nobody seemed yet to have even noticed me, except Vito, who now instructed me in the kind of pose he wanted me to adopt, which was one of standing and leaning slightly back against some large wooden boxes. When he was satisfied, he turned on an electric heater directed at me from the foot of the platform, and then went off to busy himself in the supply-room.

Gradually, they started in to work. They looked me over, but they never looked me in the eye. They talked frequently with each other, but no one said a word to me. I held my pose as well as I could, but allowed my eyes to wander around the room. It seemed that, whenever I looked towards anyone, especially the women, they would avert their gaze. After a while, I began to realize that I was not feeling at all embarrassed. In fact, I was rather enjoying the situation.

When the coffee-break came, I re-donned my gown and got some refreshments; but still, nobody came over to talk with me, and I was almost glad to get back to "work." It did not seem too long before the evening had come to an end.

"You did pretty well for a beginner," said Vito, as he paid me my six dollars. "How did you like being a model?"

"Fine," I said, departing, "but I never felt so ignored in my life."

Claremont, California 1957

Outage

It was about 10:30 in the morning when our lights went out for the first time. Then they kept coming back on and going back off again, together, of course, with our electric clocks, the VCR, the telephone-answering machine, the computer, and everything else that draws nourishment and sustenance from the numerous electric teats implanted within our walls.

I was alone in the house. Instinctively, I sought comfort from my fellow-mortals. Rushing outside to the nearest habitation, I soon found that my neighbors were similarly afflicted. Wonderful! This is no visitation directed merely upon me and mine, nothing for which I personally am in any way responsible. There was nothing I need do but go home and wait for everything to return to normal.

The telephone, I found, was still working. The operator told me that many people had already been trying to call Southern California Edison. Obviously, a larger area than just my neighborhood had been affected. Better and better! We are all in this together! Great forces, over which we as individuals have no control are deciding our destiny in this crisis. We must have faith in whatever gods may be at S.C.E.

It was all over in about fifteen minutes. The lights came back on, and stayed on. Apart from having to re-set a few clocks, I was unscathed by the event. So I thought, at least, until the next day, when I learned what had caused it. Two men flying in the area in a helicopter had clipped a power-line and crashed. They had both died. The flickering of my lights had been the ending of their lives.

Once I lived in San Francisco, near the eastern end of Golden Gate Park, in a district called the Haight-Ashbury. It was during the turbulent late Sixties, when disturbances of all kinds were almost routine in that area. One day we heard a loud bang coming from the direction of the Park. We went on with our dinner. Later there was an explanation in the news. A bomb had been thrown into the Park Police Station. A policeman had been killed.

Hearing the sound was the extent of my involvement. But hearing the sound made me to that extent a witness. And being a witness made me to that extent a participant in the event. Ask not for whom the bell tolls. Ask not for whom the lights flicker. We are all in this together.

Santa Barbara 1989

Bits and Pieces

Lust in the Dust

I saw two bugs
In close embrace
On a public path—
A sheer disgrace!

June 1980

A Two-Word Poem

Why
Die?

Dcember 1988

Bond

I glued the cracks in my bathtub with superstrong cement. When the earthquake came, the house fell down, but the bathtub remained intact. My wife and I lost interest in each other years ago, but we stay together for the sake of the bathtub.

San Francisco, June 1965

Just My Luck

I probably won't ever win the Lottery. My chances of doing so, I must admit, are not improved by the fact that I never play it. But I'm not a gambling type by nature, and in the case of our State Lottery the odds seem so ridiculously unsporting that the huge prizes don't even tempt me. This, however, does not mean that I'm not interested in the whole thing. In fact, I view it with great interest and smiling approval.

To me, it seems almost too good to be true to have what is in effect a non-compulsory tax which benefits everybody (at least in theory) and which millions of people pay quite willingly, often even claiming to feel that they are having "fun" while doing so. Why did we take so long to institute such a boon to our society?

There are, of course, still some who are appalled at the spectacle of sudden great wealth falling upon totally "undeserving" recipients. But such critics entirely fail to appreciate the true mystique of these proceedings. Our culture has in many ways been based on the idea of having others endure all kinds of unpleasantness on our behalf. It must go back at least as far as the ancient Hebrews, who used to drive an animal—a "scapegoat," supposedly bearing all their sins—out into the wilderness to perish.

In our own time, we are still, from an early age, immersed in tales of patriots and pioneers, saints and saviors, who in various ways are supposed to have suffered for our sake. Presumably none of these fine people deserved their misfortunes any more than the poor goat did. Embroidering upon this questionable tradition, Shirley Jackson even wrote a famous short story called, "The Lottery," in which a modern community has evolved where for no known reason an annual event takes place which consists of the stoning to death of some totally innocent citizen, chosen by lot.

But here in our own real Lottery, we happily have the opposite principle at work: instead of pain and misery, we take a lucky few and, in the name of all of us, heap upon them enormous good fortune. Like the Dalai Lama who is selected at birth from an entire nation by spiritual means to be the venerated leader of his people, our lottery winner finds himself or herself elevated by pure chance into the possession of great riches—an almost miraculous occurrence in which the rest of us can at least share vicariously. What a civilized concept! It is the ultimate in democracy combined with the ultimate in privilege.

What troubles me, however, is that the big winners never seem to be the kind of people with whom I personally can identify. Not that I have any objection to all the happiness that money can buy going to an elderly retired waitress or an unschooled immigrant construction worker. Such people (according to the interviews) usually have their own quite understandable plans for spending their bonanzas on family, fun, and fantasy fulfillment. But their plans are never anything like what mine would be if I were in their shoes. Why can't the jackpot ever go to somebody with my kind of background and values—somebody I feel I can trust to use the money just as wisely as I would have used it myself?

Alas, I am forced to conclude that people as wise as that don't tend to play the lottery. It's a pity. They really should.

Santa Barbara 1990

Get the Point?

There are only two kinds of hotel in the world: those that hardly matter, and those where you find your first sheet of toilet paper folded to a neat point. I have often wondered whose mind first conceived the need for this particular service, and in just what way it is intended to add to the comfort or safety of the guest. I speculate that some day I will undo the fold and find inside some little gift from the management, or at least a few words of appreciation or inspiration.

But no, that little convergence is apparently intended to convey its own message. What can it be? Since the direction of the point is always downward, towards Mother Earth, is it some profoundly existential statement about our roots and our destiny? Or are we meant, sitting there, to be joyfully contemplating the ultimate meeting of parallel lines and the grandeur of our place in the cosmos?

I wonder too just what instructions are given in the course of their training to those (usually ladies) who perform this service. Is there some rigidly-enforced standard of toilet-paper pointing, or is it left to each housekeeper's creativity? I have never been present to witness the act, but I like to imagine it as the triumphant finale in the servicing of my room—the last bold step which sets the seal upon the whole operation. When all the cleaning, changing, and straightening is finished, she stands there taking one careful critical look all about; then, and only then, if nothing else remains undone, *it is time to point the toilet-paper!* With practised dexterity she makes the little folds, perhaps at the same time kneeling and uttering some secret mantra. Then at last, possibly with a departing bow towards the bathroom, she slips away, confident of having offered her own small proof, however we may interpret it, that life need not be entirely pointless.

Santa Barbara 1990

Pot-Shots

BY ASHLEIGH BRILLIANT

© ASHLEIGH BRILLIANT 1981.

POT-SHOTS NO. 2241.

SOME OF MY TROUBLES ARE SO FAMILIAR,

I KNOW THEM BY THEIR FIRST NAMES.

Ashleigh
Brilliant

Black Snow

While sharpening some of our pencils today, I came upon one imprinted with my wife's maiden name, Dolly Tucker. Her real name is Dorothy, but she was always known to her family as Dolly. When I showed her the pencil, she remembered that it had been one of a set given her by an aunt, but she had never taken them to use at school, because at school she was called Dorothy, and the "Dolly" was something of an embarrassment.

This put me in mind of a time when as a child I somehow came into the possession of some pencils which had once belonged to my Uncle Neddie. They had never been used, or even sharpened, and were in their original leather case. Only now did I understand the likely reason. He was always known to everybody as Ned or Neddie. But the pencils were imprinted with his real name, Nathan Adler.

Uncle Neddie was a great kidder. During World War II, he was in the Canadian Air Force. I was then about eight years old and living in Washington, D.C., and he sent me a letter saying that, where he was stationed, the winters were so long and dark that they got black snow. To prove it, he enclosed a "sample"—a little packet of cut-up pieces of black paper.

Uncle Neddie died a few months ago in Ottawa, but I hadn't seen him for years. The last time was when he came on a brief visit to Los Angeles, and that was the first time in about 20 years. In those 20 years, I had succeeded in getting my immediate family to stop calling me "Junior," the name by which, for some strange reason (my father's name being Victor) I had been known all through my childhood. But to Neddie I was still Junior, and I had to make a special point of asking him not to call me that any more. To which he replied, "O.K., Junior."

Somehow, it never occurred to me, until I saw my wife's pencil this morning, that I should have come back with "O.K., Nathan!"

Santa Barbara, August 16, 1980

49

POT-SHOTS NO. 588

I may be gone tomorrow,

but that won't mean

that I wasn't here today.

© BRILLIANT ENTERPRISES 1974.

That's (Life)

In the book of time (and in many other books), the name
of every person who has ever lived is always followed by a
pair of parentheses. Inside them are usually a couple of
dates separated by a hyphen. In various reference works
which I consult, this little device has a habit of popping up
somewhat abruptly. Thus, for example, instead of simply
saying "Jack Benny, the famous comedian...," the passage
will read "Jack Benny (1894-1974), the famous comedian...,"
reminding me that somebody who may have been making
me laugh on TV just a few minutes ago, and who, for me,
can never really die, now indeed belongs to the ages.

Of course, these parenthesized dates do serve the useful
purpose of pinning the person down for us historically, and
they enable us (if so inclined) to play the little game of
calculating how old he or she lived to be. But they also
have a certain tombstone-like aspect which, when in the
right (or wrong?) mood, I sometimes find slightly jarring. It
is not always pleasant to be confronted by so intrusive a
reminder of everybody's mortality. This can particularly be
true when the name is that of someone still living. In that
case, of course, the second date is missing. But the
parentheses are still there.

It can be even more disconcerting if, as occasionally
happens, the person in question happens to be oneself, and
I come upon the following: "Ashleigh Brilliant (1933 -)."
No hyphen in the world says more to me than that one.
There it is, just dangling in front of that gaping space,

which somehow seems to be just waiting (patiently or impatiently?) to be filled in.

There are also anomalies in this dating system. If the subject is living, but the date of birth is for some reason in doubt, we get something like "Zsa Zsa Gabor (? -)." And in cases of missing persons, there are those poignant question marks on the other side of the hyphen, as in: "Amelia Earhart (1898- ?)." But as we go farther back in time, where written records become more scarce, the parenthetical epitaph of most people must inevitably consist simply of "(? - ?)."

Sometimes our ignorance about an exact date is masked by preceding it with the Latin *"circa,"* meaning, *"about."* But there is one other little scholarly device which I personally find more soothing. It is another Latin word which is used in cases where all we know is that the person was "active" during a certain period. The word is *floruit* (commonly abbreviated to "fl."), which means "he (or she) flourished." It often appears in connection with people who are known to us only by the works of art they may have left behind. Thus, for one maker of exquisite French miniatures, we have "Jean Colombe (fl. 1467-86)"—those being the dates of his only known paintings.

I like *floruit*. It seems to say "what matters is not when you were born or when you died, but that somewhere in between you actually lived." If we must all spend our time imprisoned inside parentheses (and I am still hoping that science will someday, somehow get us out of them) the simple statement that at least we once flourished there, may, in the long run, be the best epitaph that any of us can reasonably hope for.

Santa Barbara 1990

Two Parodies

Parodies are fun, but only if you know what they are making fun of. In this case, I have to hope that you are familiar with Robert Frost's poem "Mending Wall," and with "The Bells" of Edgar Allen Poe. Otherwise, I fear that, as far as you are concerned, it will be just another sad case of Parodies Lost.

Vending Haul

Something there is that doesn't love a safe-cracker,
That creaks the silent floor-boards under him,
And spills the loot when he is on the run;
And makes policemen eager to arrest.
The work of burglars is another thing:
I have come after them to do a job
Where they have not left one drawer in a chest,
But they would have the jewels out of hiding,
Rummaging about like hogs. My work is clean,
Nobody knows about it, no one sees a thing,
Until they need the stuff and find it gone.
I let my neighbor know, his name is Bill,
And on a day we meet to make the deal,
And square it all between us once again.
We keep the loot between us as we talk.
To each the profit each deserves to get.
And some are diamonds, some so big and bright
We have to keep remembering they are hot:
"I can't sell these until the heat is off."

We almost burn our fingers handling them.
Oh, just another kind of indoor game,
One on a side. It comes to little more:
Friends as we are, we do not need to stall:
He's a good man and I stick by a bargain.
It wouldn't pay to try a double-cross,
We're both in the same boat, I tell him.
He only says, "Good neighbors make good fences."

Claremont, California 1957

The Balls

Hear the rackets with the balls—
  Tennis balls!
What a world of merriment their melody recalls!
  How they bounce, bounce, bounce,
    On the green and grassy court
  While the sun burns down with power
  Onto every leaf and flower
    — What a fascinating sport!
  In the beat, beat, beat,
  Of the searing summer heat,
While the semi-apathetic watchers lean against the walls
  Watching balls, balls, balls, balls
    Balls, balls, balls—
Watch the bouncing and the trouncing of the balls.

  Hear the rolling of the balls—
    Bowling balls!
What a world of wonderment their gravity enthralls!
  How they rumble, rumble, rumble
    Down the shiny bowling lane—
  You must never stop or stumble
  With your body or your brain
    As you bowl, bowl, bowl,
    With your heart and with your soul
For the sake of every skittle that inevitably falls
  To the balls, balls, balls, balls
    Balls, balls, balls—
To the crashing and the bashing of the balls.

  Hear the pinging of the balls—
    Ping-pong balls!
What a world of happiness their rhapsody recalls!

In a large and hollow room
How they banish all the gloom
As they echo to the impact
    Of a chop;
What a sweet stacatto soars
To re-echo on the ceiling and the floors
    Till they stop;
Bounding from a table flat,
What a happy way of giving tit-for-tat
    With a pat
    Of your bat
Your opponent murmers "Drat!"
And you know that that is that;
You have won another battle
With the balls, balls, balls,
With the balls, balls, balls, balls,
    Balls, balls, balls—
With the whacking and attacking of the balls.

San Jose, California 1958

Bad Grief

It shouldn't be necessary to do this, but I feel the time has come when somebody needs to say something against grief and grieving. Lately these topics have been getting a very positive press. The word has gone out far and wide from highly qualified experts that, at least in certain circumstances, it is O.K. to be acutely unhappy for extended periods of time. Assuming you have something legitimate to be grief-stricken about, we are told, it is a good and healthful kind of behavior, a sort of "work" you have to do, an important part of your recovery from losing whomever or whatever it is you have lost.

I say it ain't so. What I observe when I see people going through grief, mourning, or whatever else you want to call it, is people wasting time. I know whereof I speak, because I myself have already been through it a couple of times in my life—once when my father died, and once (more severely, and for a longer time) when a four-year relationship ended. Nobody can tell me that all that weeping and depression, that dwelling upon the loss, those feelings of anger and guilt and regret, which often made it impossible to concentrate upon anything else, were truly necessary or beneficial. If you add up all the person-hours lost by everybody thus afflicted, the cost to society in terms of productivity must be truly staggering.

What I say is that grief is itself a sickness, and that instead of teaching people to expect and accept it, we ought to be developing ways to get rid of it, just as we have conquered other crippling diseases. As things currently stand, I can only speculate as to what that might entail. As far as treatment is concerned, since it all happens in the brain, drugs, hypnosis, anaesthesia, and even brain surgery will probably play a part—as no doubt they already do in extreme cases. But I also favor what might be called "manipulation of the environment." The grieving person should if possible immediately be removed from his or her customary surroundings and placed in some completely different situation where there are no unfortunate reminders of the past, but plenty of new challenges and stimuli—for example, some kind of "grief camp" where the emphasis is on constant new physical and mental activity.

Ultimately, however, we must think in terms, not of treatment, but of prevention. Obviously we have a long way to go in a society which still leaves most of us so unprepared for so many of the most common types of losses. What we really need is some kind of "vaccine" against grief. This could take many forms, but the key must lie in detoxifying the concept of "loss" itself. Already technology seems to be pointing us in the right direction. If you could ask people 200 years ago what the death of a loved one would mean, you might get an answer like "I will never hear his voice again," or "I will never see her face again." The modern development of sound and video recording has changed all that. It is now theoretically possible to record every moment of a person's life, and after they die you could spend the rest of your own life playing it all back. Like just about everything else, death, even though it may still be hanging around, is not what it used to be.

That may be one reason why extensive and expensive formal mourning is no longer as fashionable as it once was (which has no doubt been a cause of great mourning in the undertaking industry). Of course, we are not yet ready altogether to stop being sorry when people, pets, or love affairs die. But we are increasingly unsure just what it is that we are sorry about. In a way, I suppose that can make the situation even more distressing. With all sorts of medical miracles here and on the horizon, death too is perhaps just another of the old certainties which we may have to let go of.

So if you must grieve, go ahead—I can't stop you, and I probably won't be able to stop myself when the next occasion arises. But while we're grieving, let's spare a few tears for poor old Grief itself. I'm sure its days are numbered.

Santa Barbara 1990

Formal Affair

Just before the execution, they brought a form for me to sign. "What's this?" I asked. "It's a consent form," they said.

"What! You want me to sign a form consenting to my own execution!"

"We would prefer it," they said. "It simplifies our book-keeping."

"And if I refuse?"

"We will, of course, proceed anyway, but we would still prefer to have your consent."

"Well, I jolly well won't consent to any such thing. In fact, I'd like it to go on record that I specifically object to being executed."

"That can also be arranged. Bring him the protest form." They brought it, and I signed with a great sense of satisfaction.

Los Angeles, June 1965

Confidentially

Yes, I have lived a little bit too long,
And I have seen a few too many things go wrong,
And I am past all hope to be inspired,
And frankly, darling, I am getting tired.

Orange, California April 1966.

Questions and Answers

Q. What is life?

A. A combination of X's, Y's, and Z's. (The words don't yet exist.)

Q. Is there life on other worlds?

A. Of course.

Q. What will happen to me when I die?

A Invalid question.

Q. What are the limits of Artificial Intelligence?

A. None whatsoever.

Q. Is there a Fifth Fundamental Force?

A. It depends who's counting.

Q. Does everything have a purpose?

A. If anything does, everything does.

Q. What is the connection between the Macrocosm and the Microcosm?

A. You.

September 1987

Going Down
in History

I will never forget how to spell SEPARATE, because getting it wrong on one occasion in grade school knocked me out of a spelling bee. When I put an E in the middle instead of an A, the teacher said, "Remember, there is A RAT in SEP-A-RATE," and that nasty RAT has stayed in my mind ever since.

But it took a more embarrassing mistake some years later to impress another fact indelibly upon me—this time a piece of history. It happened on January 18, 1955, when I was in my final year as a student at the University of London, where I was actually majoring in History. On that night I was in the London studio audience of a big Radio Luxembourg quiz program called "Double Your Money." Unlike the B.B.C., Radio Luxembourg, a commercial enterprise, was able to award large cash prizes. On this particular show you could win over 300 pounds. To me, that was a fortune—more than twice as much as my government grant for the whole year.

The quiz contestants were selected beforehand from the studio audience, by answering preliminary "test" questions. When the category of History was announced, I put up my hand, and felt very excited when I was actually chosen to be given a chance. In order to get on the program, I only had to answer one question, which was: *Which King of England Had the Longest Reign?*

This question was more tricky than it appeared. If it had asked which *monarch* of England had the longest reign, that would have been easy. Everybody knew (or at least would have guessed and been right) that it was Queen Victoria, who was Queen for sixty-four years (1837-1901). But which *king*? That was much less on the tip of anybody's tongue, especially mine just then. Feeling sickeningly uncertain, I said Henry the Third. It wasn't a bad guess, since he did reign for fifty-six years (1216-1272). But I was wrong, wrong, wrong, and all my dreams of dazzling wealth departed. The correct answer was *George the Third*, who theoretically reigned for sixty years (1760-1820). True, he was totally mad for the last nine of those years, and his son, who eventually became George the Fourth, had to be officially installed as Prince Regent in 1811. But I was too crushed even to think of appealing on this technicality.

So I didn't even get on the program. As it turned out, if I had, I would definitely have won the 300 pounds, for I knew the answers to every one of the other History questions they asked. Fame and fortune would have been mine that night, if only mad old George the Third had not hung on for such a damnably long time. I can't forgive him for that—but I also can't forget him. (You would think he had already done enough harm by causing the American colonies to separate.—A RAT indeed!!)

Santa Barbara 1990

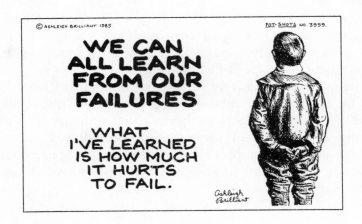

Breeched Victor

The diary I inherited from my paternal grandfather, which he had kept when he himself was a young Engish father in the early years of this century, contains a curious entry for one particular day. It reads in its entirety:

"Breeched Victor."

When I first came across this, I was baffled. "Victor" was the name of my father, then a young child. But I was not familiar with any verb "to breech." Could it have been a misspelling for "breached"? But what would *that* mean? It sounded drastic, and possibly painful.

A dictionary soon relieved my worries, at least to some extent. There is indeed a verb "to breech," although it has now fallen into disuse. On the day in question, my father had been subjected to nothing more stressful than being *put into breeches*, i.e. clothed in some kind of pants, evidently for the first time. If any stress was experienced, it was no doubt on the part of his mother, who was, to that extent, "losing her baby." What had he worn until then? Probably what most other infants of either sex wore in those late-Victorian days: a little dress. Getting "breeched," like getting your first hair-cut, was one of the rites of passage for every male child—and certainly worth an entry in your Pa's diary.

What a long way we have come! Not only do we no longer use "breech" as a verb, but the donning of a garment which separately encases each leg no longer indicates anything significant about either the age or the sex of the person involved.

Nevertheless, we still make quite a to-do, at least in certain situations, about just how much of the leg is covered. I myself, living in an area famous for its benevolent warmth, am, even so, considered somewhat eccentric because I prefer to wear shorts most of the time. And in other places, on at least a couple of occasions in my life, I have suffered my own stress through not being properly breeched.

My wife (who has a mercilessly long memory), still cringes with embarrassment recalling a time over twenty years ago in Rio de Janeiro when we went out to a movie together, but were denied admission because I was wearing shorts. I am not easily thus daunted. We happened to have our plastic raincoats with us, so I withdrew to an alcove, where with some difficulty I inserted my legs through the arms of my coat. Then, clutching the rest of it about me, I presented myself to the management to show that my flesh was now properly concealed. Somewhat to my surprise, thus "decently" clad, I was grudgingly permitted to waddle into the theater.

An even more dramatic incident was brought to mind when the regional British Consul-General appeared in our community recently to make a speech. As a native Briton, I was offered the honor of introducing him, and in doing so I recalled how as a teen-ager in 1952, while hitch-hiking alone in Spain, I was given a ride into the center of Madrid, where I was astonished to be promptly arrested for what I learned was then the crime of wearing shorts in a public place. Since I had no long pants with me and couldn't afford to buy any, I might be in a Spanish jail to this day, had I not been allowed to appeal by telephone to the British Consul, who sent to my rescue a liveried consular servant, arriving in an official limousine, and bearing, neatly draped over his arm, a pair of somebody's old brown trousers.

I never found out whose trousers they had been, and I was never asked to pay for them. But they got me out of jail, and they made me proud to be British. Now, nearly forty years later, it was good to be able publicly to shake the hand of the Consul-General and thank him for that one great service his colleague and Government had done me. Unfortunately, I had not saved the trousers, or I would have made the most of this formal opportunity to hand them back.

The whole occasion, as it happened, was fortuitous. Somebody else was originally supposed to deliver the introductory speech, but had been called away, and I had been asked as a replacement. Of course it meant I had to be suitably attired. But this was one time when I was quite happy to step into the breech.

Santa Barbara 1990

What's the Big Idea?

One question I'm most often asked is, "Where do you get your ideas"? As far as this chapter is concerned, the answer is simple: From a stockpile which I've been accumulating for many years on little bits of paper. As with much of my other work, I've never known what to do with them. They are all original (although, of course, for all I know, somebody else may very well have had the same idea and may even already have put it into practice). Some may be quite valuable. But I'm tired of keeping them to myself, so if you can use any of them, please do. (Just be honest about where *you* got the idea!)

❖ A joke-book in which all the jokes are carefully explained, for people with a poor sense of humor.

❖ An "Artists' Exchange" for second-hand art supplies.

❖ A jacket or other garment designed in the form of a kangaroo, with the animal's pouch being a real pocket.

❖ A "Town Crier" who really cries, i.e. weeps, for whomever or whatever needs weeping for.

❖ Dolls with teeth which children can brush, floss, etc., to learn about dental hygiene.

❖ An amusement "Theme Park" based on letters, words, and numbers. Could include very large letters of the alphabet and numerals, for children to go inside, climb, and play on.

❖ A new holiday: *Forgiveness Day*.

❖ Set *jokes* to music—turn funny stories into funny songs.

POT-SHOTS NO. 4435.

NO WONDER
MY
NEW IDEA
SEEMED
SO GREAT ~

IT'S
THE SAME ONE
I HAD
TWENTY YEARS AGO.

© ASHLEIGH
BRILLIANT
1988.

Ashleigh
Brilliant

❖ I.Q. tests for dogs and cats. Also "Rent-a-Pet."

❖ A book: *Down in the Dumps: Great City Dumps of the World.*

❖ An organization called "Worriers Anonymous."

❖ A group to counter the "Jews for Jesus" called "Kosher Christians."

❖ An American folk-opera about cars and driving.

❖ A *mechanical hug* modelled from life, so you can get the same hug, even when the "model" can't give it in person.

❖ Artificial wilted flowers.

❖ A new airline system which works like the notably efficient United Parcel Service: All passengers, regardless of where headed, are first flown to one central point, where they are sorted, then trans-shipped to their final destination.

❖ Professional *praisers*, for people who need more praise than they are getting.

❖ Utilize large roofs near large airports for advertising visible only to people in airplanes.

❖ A song called "Our Song," so that whenever it's played, people can always say, "Listen, they're playing 'Our Song'!"

❖ For people concerned about their posture: a device to wear on their heads to indicate when they are standing correctly.

❖ A door made especially for slamming in anger.

❖ A *sympathy center*, where you can go just to get unconditional sympathy when you need it.

❖ A double soccer game: four teams, two balls. Games are completely separate, but on the same field at same time. Part of the skill involved is in avoiding those playing the other game.

❖ Folding picket signs which can be easily concealed or put away when not in use.

❖ A new kind of legal punishment: *temporary* blindness or deafness; or the temporary loss of use of an arm, leg, etc.

❖ A T-shirt with a hand printed or sewn on the shoulder, as if giving a pat, with message: "Everybody Needs Encouragement."

❖ An *Encyclopedia of Literary Instances*, giving specific characters, incidents, etc., in fact or fiction, for any point you may want to make or illustrate. E.g., examples of miserliness, corpulence, procrastination, loyalty, etc.

❖ A prize for the *Best Conversation of the Month*. (To ensure spontaneity, the conversation must be recorded without knowledge of the participants.)

❖ A sound or video tape of the laughter of famous people.

❖ A TV program called *Good Losers*, about people who have failed in various ways, but have learned to live with their failures.

❖ A new business called *Elbow Room*, catering to people's elbows (a hitherto neglected part of the anatomy). Could offer "elbowcures" (a la manicures), elbow creams, elbow garments.

❖ "Travel Ribbons" *a la* military campaign ribbons, showing which countries you've been to.

❖ A commercial enterprise offering a *Permanent Party*, so that party-lovers would always have a party to go to.

❖ Instead of giving people a watch when they retire, give them the watch when they start work, and have them formally hand it back when they retire.

❖ Why not have shipping-containers for people as well as for goods. The containers could have everything necessary for comfortable living while in transit, and could serve as living-quarters upon arrival.

❖ Adult cradles.

❖ A *Book of Local Records*, limited to a particular town, county, etc., *a la* the well-known books of world records.

Voices in My Head

I am not, by any of the ordinary criteria, a religious person. But if a law were passed requiring me to choose some object to worship, I know what it would be. As the symbol of my own personal faith, I would choose a radio head-set of the kind I put on every morning when I go jogging—the kind which consists merely of a pair of earphones, and requires no little box hooked on the belt or carried in the hand. Once you don this magical device, you can no longer see it. You can even forget that you are wearing it. All you know is that from somewhere sounds and voices are coming into your head.

Radio in and of itself has always been enough to make me believe in miracles. When I read the history of technology, I can accept everything more or less matter-of-factly until radio comes in. The telegraph was wonderful, yes, and the telephone much more so. But they both needed wires—and, even if I don't really understand electricity, I can conceive of communication somehow taking place along a wire. But radio doesn't need wires or anything else—not even air! At that point, my wonder changes into sheer awe. And when you give me an "invisible" radio set that I can take practically anywhere, when I can hear voices in my head as clearly as they were ever heard by Joan of Arc or any other supposedly "inspired" person, then I feel as close to veneration as you are ever likely to find me.

But what exactly is it that I am venerating? This little voice-box is no magic stone that I happened to find on the ground. It is of human manufacture—and that to me is the most marvelous thing about it. If my own species has already reached the point of producing such a miracle—and already making it commonplace—then assuredly we are no ordinary animals, and we have a future that is worth staying around to see and be part of.

It saddens me that I personally have taken no part in inventing the radio, or done anything else as momentous. I feel like a parasite, riding through life on other people's miracles. Marconi is one of my great heroes, and his story is to me as exalting as anything in the Bible, especially when you consider that his initial earth-shaking discovery (that Morse-code-type messages could actually be sent without wires) was made when he was only 20 years old (in 1894). But he alone did not make my voices possible. (In fact, actual voices didn't begin to be transmitted by "wireless" until about 20 years later.) Marconi was, of course, only one link in the long chain of human knowledge. It is Humanity which has pulled off this particular stunt, and if I can't take any of the credit, I can at least take a little pride in being a member of the same club.

Where all this is leading us is still unclear. But we as a species obviously have a great desire to improve ourselves through better communication with each other—and we are actually doing something about it. No other species can make that claim. The radio on my head thus becomes my symbol of all that is best of whatever I am a part of in this universe. It isn't yet perfect, but I'm sure Mr. Sony is hard at work on even mightier miracles. In the meantime, as Abou Ben Adhem might have said, regardless of how I rate in terms of loving the Lord, at least put me down as one who loves his fellow Walkman.

Santa Barbara 1988

The Four Elements

Incredible as it may now seem, educated people used to think that everything in the world was composed of just four basic materials: Earth, Air, Fire, and Water. We are much wiser today, of course—and much more confused. But the ancient sages who concocted this theory were not totally rattlebrained. When you come to think of it, those four items do seem pretty elementary—and we should certainly not forget what an important role they each still play in our everyday lives.

Earth

Earth is our name for the planet we inhabit. It is also what we call the "soil," or "dirt," which covers certain parts of it. But most of "the Earth," we are told, is not made of "earth," but of such useless and unfriendly substances as magma, a kind of molten rock. Nevertheless, the Earth is our home, and, as the old song says, there's no place like it (although, to be strictly accurate, the song should add: "as far as we know").

The Earth is a sort of ball, but unlike a basket-ball, for instance, it has nothing to bounce on. It whirls and twirls without any visible means of support, maintaining a close yet distant relationship with a big, burning, mother-ball called The Sun and with a bunch of similarly non-dribbling sibling balls called planets, all dancing around in a somewhat chaotic arrangement, which, however, is politely referred to as a "system."

73

Ashleigh
Brilliant

LIVING ON EARTH MAY BE EXPENSIVE,

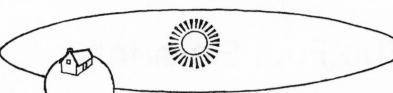

BUT IT INCLUDES AN ANNUAL FREE TRIP AROUND THE SUN.

* * * *

I SMELL AIR ON YOUR BREATH:

HAVE YOU BEEN BREATHING AGAIN?

Ashleigh
Brilliant

Let's face it: Earth is not for everyone. It is an acquired taste, and for the non-Earth buff it is usually too hot or too cold or too boring. But, with all its disadvantages, it is still the only one of the four elements which offers anything you could call solid—which is a big plus for those of us who like to have something to stand on.

Air

You can't see it, and, if you can taste or smell it, something's probably wrong with it (or with you). But it's definitely there, all around the outside of you, and, on a fairly regular basis, being solemnly sucked into your inside. Wherever it is, it tends to shift about, always moving in the direction known as down-wind. It fills basketballs and bicycle tires, and without it our whole Air Force would be grounded. Today we know that it is actually a melange of gases, including such bizarre ingredients as argon, neon, helium, methane, krypton, and xenon. Unpalatable as this may seem, scientists (those weird humorists) jocularly inform us that we are walking around at the bottom of an ocean of this stuff.

Fire

Unquestionably the most exciting element, fire is like a little piece of the sun, and this explains much about the fascination of smoking, cooking, and camping, to say nothing of incinerating and cremating, and just plain arson. Life itself, say those same witty scientists, is a form of combustion—which would certainly explain those feelings so many of us seem to have had lately of being "burned out." Fire generally produces both light and heat, each useful in its way, but the major contribution of fire to civilization has probably been to provide employment in Fire Departments for thousands of men whose love of climbing ladders, smashing windows, and sliding down poles would otherwise have to be repressed, with who knows what psychological consequences.

Water

If water did not exist, somebody would have to invent it, and would probably become very rich in the process. Its basic quality, known as "wetness" is possessed by no other element, and makes it extremely useful in sticking stamps. Without water, there would be no floods, but the tourist trade would be hard-hit, and most cruises would have to be curtailed. The entire laundry industry is also based upon this substance, and it is drunk in large quantities by those animals which have not yet discovered Coca-Cola.

So, those are the four elements, and, according to the theory, you could put them together in various ways to form anything else. Today we have over a hundred elements, and, for some reason, we are still looking for more. This is progress?

Santa Barbara 1990

Bloody Good Show

I had not given blood in thirty years, so I figured it was about time. A local radio station was sponsoring a " Blood Drive" in our central Plaza, and the ads made it sound like a big party, with refreshments and prizes. But I was worried. The whole idea of being even partially drained of so notoriously essential a bodily fluid is one I find distinctly unappealing. Would it hurt? Would I faint again (as I had done last time)?

Arriving at the Plaza with considerable trepidation, I found that it had been turned for the occasion into a "M.A.S.H."-type military field hospital, complete with camouflage-netting, and all the nurses and other attendants in at least some semblance of battle-dress. Somehow, it was not at all reassuring, at such an early stage of the hostilities, to find myself already cast in the role of a casualty. My only consolation was the thought that at least they had not chosen a theme based on Dracula.

Before any carnage could take place, however, there was, of course, the paperwork. After taking my name and address, they immediately wanted me to answer a lot of very intimate questions about my sex life and social habits. I couldn't help feeling that this was not quite the right spirit with which they should be accepting my incredibly generous gift. But it was no use being indignant. Nowadays, as with the "security" at airports they obviously have to be very careful.

But then came an even more bizarre formality. You are given a special little card which you are told to fill in and drop into a certain slot like a "secret ballot." On the card, which contains your identifying number, you are asked whether you really want the blood you are about to donate to be actually used. If you say *No*, they still take your blood, but they don't use it. But why would you say *No* right in the middle of this whole operation? Only because you don't want somebody to know (including, perhaps, the people with whom you have come today), that you belong to one of the broad forbidden groups, which include all "men who have had sex with another male since 1977" and all "persons who have been heterosexual partners of a prostitute (male or female) in the last 6 months." It's sadly plain that, thanks to AIDS in particular, we live in a world in which "purity of blood" has come to have a meaning far more ominous than the Nazis could ever have conjured up in their wildest ravings.

Next came a blood-pressure reading, and simultaneously an actual finger-prick blood-test, the pricking done very fast by some evil little instrument which the nurse tells you, after she has used it, most people object to more than any other part of the procedure. I must have seemed rather hesitant while going through all this, because they kept telling me that I was perfectly free to back out. But by this time it would have required more moral courage to leave than to stay. So, grimly conscious that I was echoing the last words of Gary Gilmore, when the sticking-point came, I simply said, "Let's do it."

So, there I found myself on a beautiful Saturday afternoon, prostrate in the heart of Santa Barbara, with a needle in my arm draining away my life's blood. The only real pain I felt was psychological: What if something should happen just now to distract everybody—an earthquake, or even a car veering off the road into the Plaza—everything in chaos, with me quite literally stuck here!

It all took a rather long seven minutes, at the end of which I was still conscious, not noticeably paler or weaker, and, for whatever reason, distinctly more cheerful. Without even glancing at the presumably full blood-bag, I allowed what was left of me to be led over to the refreshment-table, where, while also gulping the mandatory juices, I for once felt free to indulge abundantly in rich cookies without any sense of guilt.

I didn't win any of the prizes, but all in all, the experience was not a bad one, and, in bidding farewell to my fellow-donors, I was able to say with considerable sincerity, "It's been a pleasure bleeding with you today."

Santa Barbara 1989

POT-SHOTS NO. 840.

Ashleigh
Brilliant

WORDS CAN NEVER EXPRESS

WHAT WORDS
CAN NEVER
EXPRESS.

Upon My Word

Words and language are the tools of my trade. But they are also my toys and my hobby. Come play with me!

«»

Be Careful What You Say!

For some reason, I like to collect certain linguistic oddities. One kind might be called Frightful Similarities, such as between

PURified and PUTrified
INcrement and EXcrement
THERAPIST and THE RAPIST

Along the same lines, we have words or expressions which can mean two completely different, even quite opposite, things. For example:

OVERSIGHT can mean either "supervision" or "mistake."

IN CHARGE OF can mean "having custody of" or "being in the custody of."

UPHOLD certainly doesn't mean the same as HOLD UP.

If my fingernails have been FILED AWAY, you may or may not find them in my filing cabinet.

And Be Careful How You Say It!

"CRIPPLE my income!—I thought you said it would TRIPLE my income!"

"UNEQUAL SERVICE!—I thought you said UNEQUAL-LED service!"

"ILLUMINATED!—I thought you said it should be ELIMINATED!"

«»

He was tried in ABSENTIA, and hanged in EFFIGY,
— but I can't find either of them on the map.

«»

Isn't it interesting how the word SECURITY has come to connote INSECURITY (as in SECURITY GUARDS) and how the word ADULT has come to connote IMMATURE (as in ADULT BOOKSTORES).

«»

CRUEL NUMBERS: sadistics

«»

Colonic Irritation

In 1950, when I was living in London, the famous and ancient ceremonial Stone of Scone was stolen from its special place beneath the Coronation Chair in Westminster Abbey. A widespread search was conducted, including dredging of the Serpentine Lake in Hyde Park, where it was thought the thieves might have dumped it.

Like most other people, I hoped that the Stone would soon be recovered, and was therefore very glad when I saw a newspaper headline which said:

"STONE SAFE: FOUND IN SERPENTINE."

Later, however, I heard a B.B.C. report that the Police were still looking for the Stone. Puzzled, I looked again at the newspaper and for the first time read the story, which told how, while searching for the Stone of Scone in the

Serpentine, the police had not found it, but had dredged up something else which somebody had mysteriously dumped: an old safe. I had mis-read the headline. What it actually said was

"STONE: SAFE FOUND IN SERPENTINE."

(The Stone was eventually returned in Scotland, its original home. I don't know if the mystery of the safe was ever solved. But for me, the whole event was punctuated with significance.)

Beyond a Joke

One fascinating thing about our language, which I have never seen discussed, is how a number of words and expressions which were originally intended as *jokes* have been incorporated quite seriously into our common speech. Two good, fairly recent examples of this are *disc jockey* and *soap opera*. The more you think about their literal meanings, the funnier they become. An older specimen is *tandem*, which is a pun on the Latin word meaning (in terms of time) "at length." Then we have *The Three R's*, which of course would be three R's only to somebody who hadn't yet learned them very well.

I can give you three other examples of jokes embedded in our language, but these need a little more explanation:

One is *shrink* for a psychiatrist. This derives from the joking idea of confusing a "head-doctor" with a head-*shrinker*, i.e. a practitioner of that no-longer-fashionable rite of actually boiling, shrinking, and preserving human heads, usually those of slain enemies.

Then there is the expression to *drop the other shoe,* meaning "to relieve suspense." I have always assumed that this comes from the old joke about the man staying in a hotel who, as he is undressing for bed late at night, carelessly drops one of his shoes on the floor. At this point he realizes that somebody may be asleep in the room below, so he takes off the second shoe carefully and lays it down very quietly. He then goes to bed and to sleep. Hours later, he is awakened by a knock on his door. It is the man from the room below, begging, *"Would you please drop that other shoe!"*

Finally, I give you (in a manner of speaking) *foot-in-mouth disease*, which is actually a rare case of one joke piled on top of another. The expression means "an habitual tendency to make very embarrassing remarks." It goes back to the old expression "to put your foot in it" (the "it" no doubt originally being some unpleasant mass of ordure on the ground), which meant "to make an embarrassing mistake." Upon this foundation, some wit at some point built the joke that said, "Every time he opens his mouth, he puts his foot in it."

Now it happens that there is a well-known disease of cattle called *foot-and-mouth disease*. And at some later inspired moment, some other genius thought of combining the two ideas to create the masterpiece of *foot-in-mouth disease*.

A Pet Peeve

I have never seen this discussed anywhere, and perhaps it doesn't bother anyone else, but I am infuriated by what I call the *double is*. It occurs very commonly in American speech, often in that of well-educated people. It consists of an extra, redundant, *is*, inserted usually after a legitimate *is*, and appears in sentences like this: "The problem with that *is*, *is* that I already have a date tonight."

Nothing, I suppose, can be done about this. Not even an act of Congress would help. But I'm glad I finally got it off my chest.

Easy as Spy

The English language is notoriously full of traps for the non-native speaker. The most dramatic illustration of this I know is a true incident of World War II, concerning some German saboteurs who were landed on the East Coast of the United States. They had been specially chosen for their knowledge of English and their ability to pass themselves off as Americans. But one of them, in talking to a real American, immediately aroused suspicion when he happened to describe the bright sunlight as being "a sight for sore eyes" (when he clearly meant that it made the eyes sore). This soon led to the capture of the entire group, and several were executed—so, in a very real sense, that little misuse of an idiom proved fatal.

«»

Some Original Malaprops

She's home, watching terror-vision.
He was taken to the hospital, and given insensitive care.

«»

Game of the Name

Don't ask me why, but every so often I find myself thinking up funny names. For example, how about:

A company called BOGUS VULTURE BLEMISH ASSOCIATES.
A English village called UPPER SNARLING.
Mr. and Mrs. ARSON GUTSCRATCH.
Dr. MARSH QUAGMIRE and Dr. PELLAGRA PITFALL.
The law firm of HUNG, DRAWN, AND QUARTERED.
PLETHORA PRODUCTIONS INC.
A hair-cream called GUMPTION.
A new beverage called BREW-HA-HA.
Lake WASHACATPAN.
A dog named SALIVA.

I'M NOT GETTING PAID MUCH
FOR STAYING ALIVE

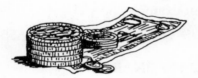

BUT IT'S GOOD EXPERIENCE

Ashleigh
Brilliant

A Thought
for Your Pennies

There used to be a legend that the streets of America were paved with gold. I do a lot of walking and bicycling around my town, and I can tell you that in recent years this is one legend which has almost literally come true. Everywhere I go, there is money—actual cash—lying in the street, just waiting to be picked up. This is such an amazing phenomenon (and for some reason so little reported on) that several years ago I began to keep a careful record of every find I made. The time has come to publish these remarkable statistics. (My raw data, and the actual currency found, are available for scholarly inspection.)

Between September 1, 1986 and June 18, 1991, I made no fewer than 273 separate street-money findings. Most were of single coins or bills, but occasionally there would be a multiple strike, such as the two nickels and five pennies all found in the same area on August 29, 1990. The most common find was that of a single penny, of which I found a total of 238, many of them heavily scarred, indicating a long time of lying in the road before being rescued. There were 27 nickels, 42 dimes, and 11 quarters, but no coin larger than a quarter. In paper money, I found five one-dollar bills (three in a multiple strike), one five, and one ten-dollar bill. The grand total comes to $30.68.

I must emphasize that, unlike the people you sometimes see hopefully sweeping the ground with metal-detectors, I have never gone out looking for money. All of these finds were purely accidental. On the other hand, I have made it a point never to overlook a possible find, even if it meant dismounting from my bicycle amid traffic and going back to pick up a penny I thought I saw in the road. (I have had to make an exception to this rule, however, in the case of numerous coins which are stuck in road-tar and too difficult and messy to remove. A fortune is waiting for somebody with the courage to perform these challenging extractions—and the patience to remove the tar from the money and themselves afterwards.)

It thus appears from my figures that over a period of nearly five years, I have been serendipitously enriching myself at a rate approaching two cents a day. This may not seem staggering to you—but consider the implications. If one person can find two cents every day of the year, without even trying very hard, then a million people could easily find $20,000 a day. If we could motivate a substantial portion of our total population, say 200,000,000 people, to interest themselves in this project, they could be finding as much as $4 million a day, or nearly a billion and a half dollars a year! Surely I need not stress the impact this could have upon our entire national economy.

At this point, the question naturally arises, how did all this money get onto our streets in the first place? You might assume that, in order to be found, it first has to be lost. But not necessarily. The great preponderance of pennies in my trove makes me suspect that another factor is at work: pennies have come to be regarded as of so little value that people don't lose them any more—they simply no longer bother to pick up the ones they accidentally drop in the street.

This attitude surprises me—and not only because of those proverbial assurances that a penny saved is a penny earned, and that the pounds will take care of themselves if we only take care of the pennies. Of course I know it's hard to find anything you can buy for a single penny nowadays. But there is one object still priced at only one cent which seems to me an amazingly good value. It is an historically significant artifact in the form of a small copper disk, beautifully engraved on both sides with words, images, and symbols. It is—*the penny itself!*

Surely if you consider the metallic content alone, this is a case of gross under-pricing. And when you add all the value created by making this little piece of specie into such an attractive object, for which so many practical and ornamental uses can be found, the American penny, at 100 for a dollar, must today be one of the best bargains in the world. This situation, of course, cannot last. Sooner or later, people are going to realize that, instead of besprinkling our streets with these charming little tokens, they should be saving them against the inevitably approaching time when pennies will be withdrawn altogether from circulation.

I myself am certainly going to hoard the ones I find. And I would probably set about getting as many more as I could from the banks, if I had the storage space—and if I could figure out a way to prevent my floor from collapsing under the weight. But even so, I have to tell you that if you choose to hoard pennies, you must do so because you love them for their own sake, and not from any hope of financial gain. Because even if they cease to be legal tender, there's no guarantee that their value will soar anytime soon.

I learned this when I visited a local coin dealer's store recently, and checked a few prices. I found that you can still buy a genuine ancient Roman coin, minted as long ago as 2000 years, for as little as $8—a sum which might actually buy fewer loaves of bread today than you could have bought back then for the same coin (not to mention that the bread might not even be as good today).

So don't hold your breath waiting for your pennies to appreciate in value. It may be that their only real worth, even 2000 years from now, will be as part of the historical record, to tell the people of the future about our civilization. But even then, I'm not sure what anyone living 2000 years from now will conclude about us, if their only evidence is one of our pennies. Very likely, they will get us confused with the Greeks and Romans, since our penny has on one side what looks like a Greek temple, together with some words in Latin. As for that fellow on the other side with the beard, crowned by the words, *In God We Trust*— well, obviously, he must have been our deity.

So I have to admit that it may not make much sense either financially or historically to go on scooping up pennies off the public thoroughfares. And even in the case of larger denominations, we all know that their days are numbered too. Surely it can only be a matter of time before an all-credit economy puts "paid" to our whole anachronistic system of metal and paper money.

But there is also an ecological factor to consider here. And if my own special numismatic endeavor fails to win your sympathy in any other way, please at least give me some credit for being environmentally conscious. After all, not everybody is willing to spend so much time helping to remove this particular form of litter from our streets.

Santa Barbara 1991

The following was one of an irregular series of columns called *Trash From Ash,* which I wrote for the *Haight-Ashbury Midtown Record,* a "throw-away"-type weekly newspaper in 1967-1968.

How I Became a Hippie

When I arrived in the Haight-Ashbury about four months ago, I was undergoing an identity crisis. I didn't know who or what I was, and this was very inconvenient, especially when filling out forms. I was worried too because I had turned thirty-three, the same age as Christ when he died—and Easter was coming.

Occasionally I noticed that there were other people around me who seemed to have solved and survived their own identity crises. They were called Hippies, and, if there was one thing I was sure of, it was that I wasn't one of them. I knew I wasn't a Hippie because, if I were a Hippie, I would feel free to grow a beard, and have no hesitation in going to sit on Hippie Hill.

Around Easter-time, however, some kind of miraculous transfiguration must have taken place. I didn't find out about it until I read in the *Examiner* on April 7 that, among those who had spoken at a Haight-Ashbury Town Hall Meeting the previous evening was: "Ashleigh Brilliant, a hippie." At first I was amazed. I still had no beard. I had never sat on Hippie Hill. My clothing was drab and ordinary. All I had done at the meeting was recommend a very moderate reform in the drug laws.

But who was I to question such a source? At last I had an identity! That very day I stopped shaving, and for the first time set foot on Hippie Hill. Nobody questioned my right to be there. I didn't once have to produce my clipping. But lying there in unaccustomed peace, with my arms outstretched and Easter safely past, I thanked God for the *San Francisco Examiner*.

San Francisco, July 13, 1967

Marks on the Land

According to a story which I hope is not apocryphal, two events once occurred on the same day in a certain Midwestern town: an abandoned ice-house burned down, and a society matron died. The local newspaper featured both stories on its front page, but somehow got the headlines mixed up, and the photograph of the deceased matron appeared with the heading: OLD EYESORE GONE AT LAST.

Much as I love that story, I have to admit that the question of just what constitutes an "old eyesore," as opposed to a "landmark" worthy of preservation for all time, is one about which I have many doubts and misgivings. It seems we are constantly hearing about battles between "developers," who want to make radical changes to our familiar landscapes and cityscapes in the name of progress, and "preservationists" intent on keeping things as they are, or even "restoring" them to the way they were at some hallowed point in the past.

In general, I must say I tend to side with the preservationists, if only because they so often seem to be the underdogs, locked in unequal combat with powerful economic forces, and because what is familiar has a strong emotional appeal over what is strange and new. But it must also be acknowledged that everything our society has constructed that we enjoy today was at some point a possibly sinister-seeming "new development."

For example, take our local Alpha Beta supermarket. I

© BRILLIANT ENTERPRISES 1974

POT-SHOTS NO. 643

SOME PARTS OF THE PAST
MUST BE PRESERVED,

Ashleigh
Brilliant

AND SOME OF
THE FUTURE
PREVENTED AT ALL COSTS.

don't know what was there before it was built—possibly just trees and fields where children used to play—a lost happy world of nature and innocence. It is a world, however, which I have no wish to restore. My own happy world includes the supermarket itself, which has been there as long as I can remember. Not being of a conventionally religious turn of mind, I think of it as the nearest thing I have to a cathedral, and guiding my wagon down its dazzling aisles is as close as I come to any regular form of worship. If some developer came along and wanted to replace my Alpha Beta with a park (admittedly an unlikely scenario), I would be as upset as those Native Americans who protest that their ancient burial places are threatened by today's bulldozers. Indeed, if my own mortal remains must eventually repose anywhere, I would just as soon have it be beneath the parking lot at Alpha Beta.

We must face the fact that today's obscene developments only too often constitute tomorrow's treasured landmarks. A classic example of this may be seen in what is probably the most famous landmark in the world—the Eiffel Tower. Incredible as it may seem, this beloved symbol of Paris, when still on the drawing-boards just over a century ago, was bitterly opposed on aesthetic grounds by nearly all the leading French intellectuals of that day. (It is said that one of these opponents, after the Tower was built and some space became available within it, actually moved his office there. When an astonished friend asked why, he explained, "It's the only place in Paris where I can't see the damned thing!")

Our local City Council (perhaps awaiting the disposition of my bones) has not yet got around to declaring the Alpha Beta an official landmark. But it does take this business of landmarks very seriously, and has already voted to protect at least 48 of them, including a bandstand, a junior high school, and a large fig tree, with landmark status, which means, among other things, that they cannot be demolished unless irreparably damaged "by earthquake, fire, or act of God."

There is something admirable about these attempts to set aside certain precious features of our community as untouchable, but also something a little sad, because no law can be truly binding upon the future. Fashions inevitably change in the course of time, and one thing no law can protect anything against is a change in the law. Future generations are bound to wonder why we bothered to save some of the things we did and why we permitted others to be destroyed.

True, there are battles worth fighting, and some of these battles can be won by the good guys. But be careful before you decide who the good guys are. I still can't shake the nagging possibility that, back in the fifth century B.C., there were some anti-developer Athenians who felt that the lovely hill known as the Acropolis would be completely spoiled by building a big temple on it.

Santa Barbara 1991

Cold Cuts

The Man Who Cut Off His Mother's Head shook my hand warmly when I arrived at his home for the party. It was a big moment for me. For years, ever since giving them permission to reprint some of my works in their newsletter and thereby landing on their mailing list, I had been following the fortunes and misfortunes of this bizarre group with keen interest; but their installation was hours away in Riverside and this was the first time I had ever taken the time to attend one of their gatherings.

It was the annual Turkey Roast of the ALCOR Life Extension Society, whose members (some 145 fully paid-up and committed, with hundreds more hangers-on) call themselves Cryonicists and believe in the possible future revival of people whose bodies, or at least whose heads, have been preserved by freezing. The man greeting me was one of the founders, Saul Kent, whose own mother, by virtue of her severed head, recently became one of a claimed 13 members already "in suspension." The resulting scandal, arising from questions raised by the local authorities as to whether the 82-year-old lady was legally quite dead at the time of the operation, has been widely publicized, and has not yet entirely been put to rest. Nor indeed, apparently, has the controversial head itself, since neither Mr. Kent nor anybody else will reveal its current location.

I myself felt it hardly discreet, considering that it was our first meeting, to ask, "Where is your mother's head?" and

POT-SHOTS NO. 805.

Ashleigh Brilliant

IF I CAN
SURVIVE DEATH,
I CAN PROBABLY
SURVIVE
ANYTHING.

© BRILLIANT ENTERPRISES 1975.

confined our conversation to topics of a more general nature, such as praising the refreshments, which were indeed superb; especially the turkey, which was soon left with very little chance of cryonic resurrection.

I did, however, feel free to inquire about the head of Timothy Leary, the charismatic guru of the 60's. It was not unfortunately, there at the party, but it is, at this writing, as far as I know, alive and well, and still closely fastened to his body. As I had seen in a news report, however, Leary had recently become a "suspension member" of ALCOR, and I was interested to learn whether he had chosen to have his whole body frozen, which costs about $100,000, or only his head, at a mere $35,000.

It was more than idle curiosity, because, despite many reservations, I myself have also been thinking seriously about taking this crazy plunge. But I find that, despite the price differential, I have strong feelings of attachment, not just to my head but also to the vast majority of my nether parts. Besides, those future scientists upon whose dedication and goodwill this entire scheme depends, would surely prefer the relatively easy task of curing whatever has caused my demise, to the tricky business of connecting up my head or brain with a whole new body.

A highlight of the party was an organized tour, for first-timers like me, of the small ALCOR "facility," located (rather disappointingly) in a nondescript "industrial park" several miles from the Kent home. On the way, I learned from our guide that Leary had, for whatever reasons, chosen the $35,000 "neurosuspension" as opposed to the total job. We were shown the large, shiny, metal cylinders in which the whole or partial remains of suspended members already repose in liquid nitrogen awaiting the ultra-modern equivalent of Judgment Day.

It was fascinating to see actually in operation what is still only a small beginning rich with promise. Yet, as we stood there hearing the various technicalities explained, all the fun of the day somehow seemed to evaporate. This is what it was all about. I tried to picture myself suspended there in smoggy Riverside for something like forever, instead of being about to drive home to Santa Barbara—my "widow" not being sure what to grieve over (except perhaps a departed $100,000)—frozen there, in a dingy warehouse, crammed into a tin can—perhaps in the same one with the head of Timothy Leary—waiting, waiting—our fate totally out of our hands (even more so in *his* case than in mine, since I at least would still *have* hands!) and always at the mercy of whoever controls the precious supply of liquid nitrogen, to say nothing of whoever, in the undependable shifts of time, administers the region, governs the country, or rules the planet.

It may still be all very logical, and, for those of us with no faith in any other kind of after-life, it may be, no matter how slim the chances, the only way to go. But suddenly, standing there among those cold cylinders, I felt a renewed determination to keep going in *this* life as long as possible.

Santa Barbara 1989

The Atheist's Prayer

God who does not exist,
Help me to deny thee;
Lord of the lordless,
Give me faith to have no faith,
Give me the wisdom not to understand,
And the power to doubt.

Amid this world's mysterious griefs and pleasures,
Where each enigma breeds a cult of dreams,
Where reason yields to empty explanations,
Preserve my mind from blind believing schemes.

And let me not look upward from affliction,
Nor, drugged with love, declare my joy divine—
Between the flowers and the sky,
Defend me from the demon Why;
From Cause and Purpose keep me free,
Confine my sight to what I see—
Lest I, too, bow before thy sheltering shrine.

London 1954

Me and the Famous

Although, in a certain very limited way, I myself enjoy the status of a minor-league celebrity, my own contacts with really famous people have been dismally few. In my whole life, there have been only five such occasions of any significance, and never on even one of them, despite my constant hopes, did any of the fame seem to rub off onto me. Nevertheless, since these experiences constitute my entire stock of material for name-dropping, here are the true stories.

Me and Dorothy Lamour: the Road to Whitehall

First, I must admit that it wasn't really me and Dorothy Lamour, but my father, Victor Brilliant, and Dorothy Lamour. On May 19, 1950, the day when their paths quite literally crossed, Dorothy Lamour was still a leading light among Hollywood stars, known all over the world, particularly for the trade-mark sarong which had made her a favorite pin-up of World War II, and for her series of "Road" movies with Bob Hope and Bing Crosby. My father was a 52-year-old British career civil servant—an unassuming person, and the last one anybody would expect to draw attention to himself voluntarily. Like millions of others, he commuted daily from the suburbs into London, where he worked at the Board of Trade in Whitehall.

What happened on that fateful day (as I later pieced it together) was this: While passing the House of Commons on his usual lunch-hour walk, my father saw a small crowd gathering around a woman and two men who had

Victor Brilliant makes the front pages with
Dorothy Lamour.

evidently just come out of the building. The woman was fashionably dressed, and not in a sarong, but lo and behold, it was Dorothy Lamour! Accompanied by her husband (William Ross Howard III), she had come over from America to perform at the London Palladium, and they were visiting the Houses of Parliament, being hosted there by William Teeling, the M.P. for Brighton.

Some press photographers were also present, and they asked Dorothy Lamour to walk towards them. But as she and her two escorts did so, a strange impulse seized my father, and he did something extraordinary. Instead of hanging back out of camera-range with the rest of the crowd, he deliberately moved forward, smiling slightly, and looking directly towards the photographers! I'm sure you get the picture: he himself was trying to *get into the picture!*

And he succeeded, spectacularly!! The photos appeared that night in both of London's largest evening papers, the *News* and the *Standard.* And there he was, a little behind the three principal figures, but clearly recognizable—my father, Victor Brilliant—on the front page with Dorothy Lamour!

My father lived to be 74, but this was practically the first and only time in his life that his picture ever appeared in a newspaper. Naturally it created a major sensation in our family. We knew he was pleased, because he brought home six copies of one of the papers. Of course, the captions did not identify him. He was just part of the background. But *he* knew, and *we*—my mother and my sister and I—WE knew who that mysterious fourth person was in the picture with Dorothy Lamour. And the whole episode became a family legend, upon which, over the years, we had fun embroidering all sorts of dramatic details concerning the REAL story of my father and that glamorous star. My father never confirmed or denied our teasing "suspicions." But he did admit that he had deliberately walked into the picture. And for him and for us, that in itself was really quite dramatic enough.

Me and Aldous Huxley: Eyeless in Berkeley

Everybody knows that Aldous Huxley was a very famous man of letters, who wrote *Brave New World, Eyeless in Gaza,* and dozens of other important books. But what nobody has known, until now, is that I once had a sort of personal encounter with him.

It happened in Berkeley in 1963. I was a graduate student at the University of California when Aldous Huxley came to speak there, an occasion I made sure not to miss. To me personally he was more than just a remotely great figure, because, about ten years previously, one of his books had had an important effect on my own life. It was *The Art of Seeing* in which he told about how, having been plagued with poor vision, he had been able to improve it markedly without the use of glasses, by practicing certain eye exercises.

My own vision was not nearly as bad as his. I was just slightly short-sighted, and could do without glasses most of the time. But I hated having to wear them at all, and for months I had tried to follow the exercises as given in his book. The results, however, were so paltry that eventually I gave up, and went back to wearing glasses when I needed them. But I had always felt slightly guilty about not pursuing Huxley's method, especially because, when still enthusiastic, I had written to him expressing my appreciation for his book, and to my delight had actually received a personal hand-written reply suggesting various forms of additional help I could seek, which, however, I had never followed up on.

The lecture hall was crowded, but I managed to get a seat close enough to the front to see that, although Huxley was indeed not wearing glasses, his notes were written out in huge, dark, block letters. That was something of a jolt—but more was to come. When his speech was over, I was too shy to take advantage of this opportunity to speak to him in person. But what I did do was *follow* him at a discreet distance when he left the hall.

He was alone, and nobody else seemed to recognize him.

He walked haltingly through Sather Gate and left the campus, and I continued shadowing him as he went along Telegraph Avenue, and eventually into the Lucky supermarket near Dwight Way. There, inside the market, I stood peeking around the corner of an aisle, and watched as he took out a large magnifying glass and began attempting to read the can labels on one of the shelves.

It was a sad glimpse of this tall, rugged-looking, world-famous man, very close (as it turned out) to the end of his life—especially sad for me, of course, in view of my previous conception of him as an eyesight guru. By then, however, he had turned the whole world towards another, drug-oriented, kind of vision with his book *The Doors of Perception.*

But saddest of all, perhaps, is my view of myself, hiding there in the supermarket from Aldous Huxley; because that was the end of our "encounter." I happened to live nearby; and without ever making my presence known, I just left him there with his greatness and his magnifying glass, and went home to lunch.

POT-SHOTS NO. 266

IT'S STRANGE, BUT
WHEREVER I TAKE MY EYES,
THEY ALWAYS SEE THINGS
FROM MY POINT OF VIEW.

Me and Patty Hearst: the Un-Ransomed Letter

The bizarre train of events which began with the kidnapping of 19-year-old heiress Patty Hearst in Berkeley on February 4, 1974, had a very special significance for me. It turned a piece of paper which for years had been sleeping innocently in my files into a potential ticket to my own long-awaited fame and fortune. This magic document was a fan letter I had received from the unfortunate abductee some four and one-half years earlier. I had not then known who she was, but I had kept what she sent, as I still keep all the kind comments I receive, because they are sometimes useful as testimonials, and because they give me solace.

The hand-written letter read in its entirety: "Dear Mr. Ashleigh Brilliant, Would you be so kind as to send me a sample set of your insane cards. You must be out of your mind. ... But I love it!!! Cheers, Patty Hearst c/o Santa Catalina School for Girls, Monterey, California 93940."

It was May 4, 1974, when I discovered that I had this letter—the very day a $4,000,000 offer by her father for Patty's safe return expired. She had already (apparently voluntarily) been involved with her kidnappers in a violent bank robbery, and was suddenly the most famous and notorious woman in the world.

It was, of course, very gratifying just to think of a person so celebrated (and so intensively sought) as being among my customers and admirers. (And I later learned that, not long before the kidnapping, she had worked in the greeting-card department of an Oakland store which carried my cards—so I could enjoy the knowledge that she had already not only *bought* my Pot-Shots—but also *sold* them!)

But, with my own overpowering desire to be less neglected by the world at large, I could scarcely keep all this to myself. So, over the next year and a half, while Patty Hearst went into deep cover as a fugitive, I set about deriving whatever publicity benefits I could from my very tenuous connection with her. This was an activity which eventually culminated, on the night of December 11, 1975, in a glittering event at the Waldorf Astoria Hotel in New York. It was an auction staged by Charles Hamilton, one of the world's largest dealers in "fine autographs of interest and importance." Among the items offered for sale was what the Catalogue described as a "Rare Autograph Letter .... The first letter of Patty Hearst to appear at public auction."

By that time, Patty had already been captured (three months earlier) by the FBI, and was at the beginning of her long road back through trial and imprisonment to eventual complete rehabilitation and (at least for her) a story-book happy ending. But my own little part of the story doesn't end quite so happily. The auctioning of my Patty Hearst letter did get some publicity—even a sentence in *Time* magazine. But to my chagrin, there was never any mention of *my* name in any of the reports. And, since I had set a reserve price of $1000, and nobody bid that much, the letter didn't even get sold. I still have it. Make me an offer!

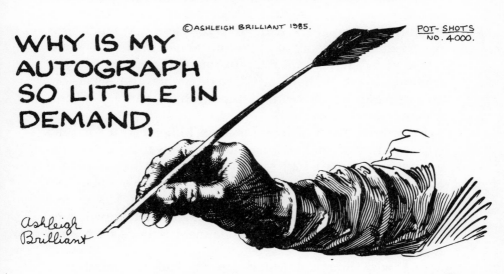

© ASHLEIGH BRILLIANT 1985.

POT- SHOTS
NO. 4000.

WHY IS MY AUTOGRAPH SO LITTLE IN DEMAND,

Ashleigh Brilliant

EXCEPT ON CHECKS?

Me and Jonathan Miller: Guaranteed Shrink-Proof

Jonathan Miller (in case his fame has not reached you) is one of the best-known modern British personalities in the fields of Theater, Literature, and Medicine. Incredibly multi-talented, he has consistently excelled as an entertainer, actor, director, and writer, besides being a highly respected physician. I have never met him in person, but for many years there has been between us a strange and (to me) uncomfortable connection. To wit: at a critical period of my own life, Jonathan Miller's father was my psychiatrist.

For seven months in 1952-53, I visited Dr. Emanuel Miller as a patient twice a week. I was 19, and in my first year as a student at University College, London. Emanuel Miller, then in his late 60's, had had a very distinguished career in psychiatry, and I would never have been able to afford him (or any other such treatment) but for the bounty of the British National Health Service, which had referred me to him, and which paid the entire cost.

I wasn't terribly sick, but I did have troubles. In particular, I was very unhappy about the fact that I had failed three times to get a scholarship to Oxford or Cambridge, and had had to settle for the much less prestigious University of London. What made this even worse was that it meant that, for financial reasons, I had to continue living at home with my parents and sister—an arrangement which by that time I had completely outgrown.

By a weird twist of fate, Emanuel Miller had a son who was just my age, and who had just been awarded one of the very scholarships I had sought in vain. (In fact, Jonathan and I took the same examination at St. John's College in Cambridge at the same time, in December 1952. His success in attaining the scholarship was probably not impeded by the fact that St. John's was his eminent father's own alma mater.)

Just why Emanuel Miller felt he had to spend time during our sessions, as he frequently did, telling me about his son's abilties and achievements, and frequently comparing me with him (invariably, as it seemed, to Jonathan's advantage), is something I have never been able to understand. It was bad enough to be compared by my own parents with other people's more charming, talented, and successful sons. I really didn't need to hear it from my psychiatrist! That was how I felt then—and that is how I still feel nearly 40 years later. But I didn't have the courage to say anything like that to Dr. Miller at the time. I just sat and listened to his proud accounts of how well his popular son was doing at Cambridge—until finally our relationship was terminated by his retirement. Not long afterwards, I emigrated to America, where you have to be much sicker to get a free psychiatrist, so I have generally managed to do without one.

But all through the years since then, it has always irritated me to have had to go on hearing, not from his father, but from the media, about the wonderful successes of Jonathan Miller, each of them greater by far than anything I have accomplished in my own life. Once, in an

POT-SHOTS NO. 539

IF YOU CARED MORE FOR MY FEELINGS,

YOU WOULDN'T BE

SO SUCCESSFUL.

Ashleigh Brilliant

© BRILLIANT ENTERPRISES 1974

attempt to exorcise this demon, I actually wrote to Jonathan Miller about it. I'm probably lucky that he never replied, because he might very well have told me that what I need is a good psychiatrist.

Me and Jimmy Carter: the Brilliant-Carter Summit

I am not ordinarily a very political animal. But once—just once—I found myself debating American foreign policy eyeball to eyeball with a President of the United States. Well, actually he was no longer President. And I have to admit that it wasn't much of a debate.

It happened on January 31, 1983, when Jimmy Carter, (defeated for re-election after a single term, and by then out of office for two years), came to speak in Santa Barbara. I was among the 1700 people who jammed our largest hall for one of the ex-chief executive's rare post-White House appearances.

After his speech, there was a question-time, and hopeful questioners began lining up at a microphone. This, I realized, was a wonderful opportunity—not only to have direct discourse with a world leader, but to be seen and heard doing so by many of the most important people in my own community. The problem was that I couldn't think of anything to ask.

So I just sat there while the proceedings went on, trying to formulate a good question on some topic that nobody else had mentioned. Eventually, one came to me, and I went up to wait my turn. But, alas, I had spent too much time thinking. The line was by then heartbreakingly long, and sure enough, before my turn came, the questioning was cut off. The whole event was officially over. I had missed my big chance to bask, however briefly, in the Presidential spotlight.

But then I saw that some shred of glory might still be salvaged. A number of people had crowded around the speaker after he left the platform. I joined them, and was able to elbow my way right up to Mr. Carter, and

THERE OUGHT TO BE A BETTER WAY THAN GOVERNMENT TO RUN THE WORLD.

Ashleigh Brilliant

eventually I got his attention. Yes, there we were, standing toe-to-toe, and I was being directly smiled at by one of the most famous faces in the world!

Of course it seemed unreal—or at least less real than seeing it on the familiar, glowing screen in my living-room. But I knew this wasn't television, because it was in color, and our TV at home was still black-and-white. In another way, it seemed more than real, as if we were on a stage together. Well, at least I knew my part. I went ahead and asked my blockbuster question.

Although I had liked some things about Jimmy Carter, one of his actions had always seemed to me a big mistake. That was his decision to boycott the Moscow Olympic Games of 1980 as a protest against the Soviet invasion of Afghanistan. I could understand his moral outrage, but what had it really achieved? Here we were, three years later, and the Russians were still in Afghanistan. Did that mean we should also boycott the next Olympic Games?

I thought this was a particularly good question, since the next Olympics, in 1984, were to be held in the United States.

I hoped it might challenge him just a little. But he gave no hint of being stunned by my audacity. Without a moment's hesitation, he simply said, "No, I don't think we should," and, instead of elaborating, he turned to answer somebody else's question.

Soon after that, he was whisked away altogether by his entourage. So that was the entire substance of my in-depth face-off with a key figure of our time. No reporters were present, and Mr. Carter himself has never publicly commented upon it. So this will probably be the only record of that historic event.

Santa Barbara 1990

Violins and Violence

I don't see much real violence in our community. When there is a stabbing or a mugging or a murder, I am usually not there. Santa Barbara is more celebrated for culture than crime, except in the pages of such cultivated crime writers as Ross MacDonald. Our restaurants are deservedly more famous than our jails. As a group, we seem to prefer mayonnaise to mayhem.

Nevertheless, it seems we do have our share of bad-mannered people, who on occasion so far forget themselves as to become the subject of very unpleasant headlines. And, because of this, we also have a police force.

I myself have what many of my friends seem to consider a strange attitude towards the police: I trust and respect them. This probably derives from my upbringing in England where as a child I was taught such precepts as, "If you want to know the time, ask a policeman." (The vision of a modern child in our town flagging down a police car to ask one of its occupants the time is almost too bizarre to contemplate.)

That was in the days before English policemen carried firearms, as I'm afraid some of them now do. For some reason, the sight of an officer wearing a gun always makes me feel at least slightly less safe than if he or she were unarmed; just as I—and, I suppose, many of us—feel less, rather than more, secure, knowing how well our country is protected by its nuclear weapons. Of course, this would not apply if the policeman were coming to rescue me from

Pot-Shots BY ASHLEIGH BRILLIANT

POT-SHOTS NO. 4108.

HOW CAN NOISY MACHINES HELP CLEAN THE WORLD,

WHEN
NOISE
ITSELF
IS
A FORM
OF FILTH?

Ashleigh
Brilliant

some situation from which only his gun could save me. But such situations, I'm glad to say, have been rare in my experience.

There was however one occasion within living memory when I myself was, at least technically, the transgressor, and the police force of Santa Barbara, fully-armed as usual, was actually summoned to deal with me, in the form of four—count them—four officers, whom I made what I later learned was the mistake of politely inviting into my house, from which it then proved much more difficult to politely get them to leave.

I knew, of course, why they had come. I had been seen removing a key from a carpet-cleaning vehicle parked in the street while servicing the house next-door to mine. The noise made by these beasts is, to my mind and ears, absolutely atrocious—and on that occasion proved intolerable. I knew from experience that it would be of no avail to attempt to register any kind of verbal plea or protest; and I had important work to do which could only be done at home. Inspecting the vehicle, I discovered a key in the motor of the cleaning mechanism. By turning this magic key, and pocketing it, I was able to restore blissful peace to the neighborhood, at least until the police arrived, summoned by the outraged operator of the outrageous machine.

This defeated my original plan, which was based on the assumption that the monster I had muted would simply retreat to its den, whereupon I could mail or deliver the key to the company, accompanied by a scathing letter. But the arrival of the constabulary required me to institute Plan Two, which was to refuse to admit guilt or even discuss the matter at issue, but simply state that I was perfectly willing to be arrested and imprisoned if this was their pleasure. It was interesting to see how they handled what was clearly a difficult and unusual situation. What they did was, several times, and with varying degrees of sternness, order me to return the key immediately.

This put me, for the first time in my life, in the uncomfortable position of refusing to obey a direct command from an armed and duly constituted Community Authority Figure. I wasn't sure exactly what my rights were in this situation, and for some reason the policemen were not very forthcoming with information on this subject when I inquired. (Apparently, it is only after they have actually decided to arrest you that they are required to tell you what your rights are.) But I had seen enough movies to recall that I had "the right to remain silent," which is what I did—and the eventual result was that, after some going back and forth, the policemen informed me that the other party had decided not to press charges, and, with very little evident emotion, they simply went away. I then decided anyway to give the key back to the miserable carpet vehicle man, who then to my great relief sped off and has not since been seen (or, more to the point, heard) in our vicinity.

There was, of course, no actual gunplay in this entire episode, and I still hope some kind of "love gas" may eventually be developed which, when necessary will enable our authorized protectors to elicit totally peaceful compliance. In the meantime, I can only be grateful, as an American, to be living in a community where the police are generally polite, efficient, and humane, and where at least the Mayor doesn't wear a gun!

Santa Barbara 1988

A Passage
from India

(Bombay was one of many ports of call for the "Floating University," a college-level educational program [now known as Semester at Sea] on board a specially-converted cruise ship on which I made two round-the-world, three and one-half month voyages as a teacher of History and Geography in 1965-67. This poem recalls the strangeness of one experience, a late-night walk back to the ship from a lavish function on shore. There was something hellish about finding the pavements covered with thousands of sheet-wrapped, sleeping people for whom that was their only home.

My companion was a young, fellow faculty member from the ship who always impressed me with his calmness even in the most extraordinary circumstances. He taught courses in Oceanography and Astronomy, and somehow, on this long, weird walk, he assumed for me the role of a guide and navigator, leading me back through some nightmare to the safety of our own world.)

You and I, good friend,
Placid oceanographer (beneath whose calm surface,
who knows what elemental torrents flow?)
Walking in the warm night of Bombay
Through streets of sleepers
cocooned upon the pavements,
Talking about the future of the Program;

You and I, fresh from the gala reception,
Picking our way among the images of death,
In Bombay, where hope is a disease;

You and I, comforting friend, finding our way
by your stars, back to your ocean.

At Sea, December, 1966

121

Pot-Shots

BY ASHLEIGH BRILLIANT

POT-SHOTS NO. 897.

©BRILLIANT ENTERPRISES 1976

SOME PARTS OF ME ARE SO PRIVATE THAT I MYSELF HAVE NO KNOWLEDGE OF THEM.

Ashleigh Brilliant

The Rite of Privacy

Please stand back. I am about to attempt to slaughter a sacred cow. The beast is called Privacy, and I am amazed at how much solemn kowtowing she still receives in our otherwise enlightened times. Frightened by fantasies of a totally controlled society, many people seek refuge at the other extreme, and seem to think we all have some God-given right never involuntarily to be electronically observed or recorded, especially by anyone in authority, and not even to have information about ourselves collected in a computer. But there is no such right—not in our Constitution or anywhere else. Nor can there be. Nor should there be.

There can't be any such right, because technology, whose advances nobody can stop, is constantly making it easier to cross any line we may attempt to draw between what is private and what is not. Of course, we all have certain needs and desires to be let alone. But we have to live in a world where, to take just one example, a long-range directional microphone, which anybody can buy, can hear "private" conversations taking place so far away that the people conversing may be completely unaware of being overheard. All sorts of other "surveillance" equipment now exists, and is being steadily improved to make it smaller, lighter, cheaper, more powerful, and more easily concealed. And, of course, all kinds of computers are readily available to organize the information thus gathered.

To attempt to ban the manufacture or use of any such

equipment would be as futile and retrograde as to outlaw telescopes and binoculars. But there is nothing really new about this "threat" (if you choose to see it as one), and perhaps you may feel a little less uneasy about it if I remind you of two earlier developments which we all now more or less take for granted, but which, in their time, successfully challenged the Rite of Privacy.

One of these victories for common sense had to do with photography and one with aviation. Incredible as it may now seem, when "candid" photography first became feasible, about a century ago, it was considered an invasion of privacy to photograph any person without his or her permission, even if that person happened to be only one member of a crowd in a public place. And a few years later, in the early days of flying, airplanes could not legally fly, at any altitude, over any private property, without the consent of the property owner, because ownership of land was considered to extend upwards from the surface of the earth to infinity.

In each case, of course, the laws had to change, and our ideas about privacy had to be scaled down. The law now assumes that by appearing in a public place, you are automatically giving anybody with a camera permission to take your picture. And, as far as flying-machines are concerned, we have given up many if not all of our individual ownership rights in the air above us in exchange for a whole new system of transportation.

Of course, there must still be safeguards. But the best safeguard against abuse of modern techniques of surveillance and information-control is not to restrict them or try to counteract them with other technological devices, but rather to disperse them so broadly that nobody has an advantage. By all means, let the government continue to amass information on everybody; but let everybody then have access to it, so that we can all, at least in theory, say, "My file on you is as big as your file on me." Let privacy become what it ought to be: a matter not of legal rights, but of custom, taste, and courtesy.

Not long ago, the editor of a London newspaper was fired for having breached a person's privacy, and, in that case, I sympathized with the victim. He happened to be Britain's young Prince William, who was seven years old at the time. The paper had published a (non-frontal) photograph of him urinating in a park, under the headline "THE ROYAL WEE." Firing may have been somewhat extreme (although in an earlier era such an offence might have incurred some more literal head-rolling), but I do think the editor deserved at least a reprimand. Why? Because, rightly or wrongly, pictures of people urinating are not ordinarily published in newspapers, and only the royalty of the subject made this one of any possible interest to any normal person. To exploit the little boy in this way just because of his family connections was simply a violation of basic decency.

But the scaling-down of privacy in general is clearly going to continue. Mere "invasion" of it will cease to be a punishable offense, unless the invaded party can prove that he or she has suffered some specific damage or loss as a result. For example, we will probably soon be legally free, if we are not already, to "bug" each other's houses, cars, and work places; even to see, without being seen, at a distance into darkened bedrooms using infra-red light, so long as it is done merely for our own personal interest and amusement and does not result in anyone being harmed.

Most of us may find this whole trend rather shocking; but I think we will learn to live with it, just as we learned to live with the "intrusions" of cameras and airplanes. And in many ways it can all be of great social benefit. For example, public shame (as used in China) can be a powerful force in controlling antisocial behavior, and if we knew more about each other's criminal records, it would probably be a great deterrent to crime. And if medical records were not so closely guarded there might be fewer situations in which desperate victims have to make pathetic appeals through the media for rare transplant material to save their lives.

The whole area of Personal Identification is one in which outdated ideas of privacy must eventually be abandoned. Many Americans are still afraid even to reveal their Social Security numbers. But all kinds of social and business activities would become easier and safer if there were some convenient system by which we could "read" and immediately identify any person on sight. This sort of thing is already being done with cattle. A farmer can have each of his cows marked with a computer-readable tag containing various statistics and other useful information about the animal. It doesn't hurt the cows and, once we get used to the idea, a similar system for people probably won't hurt us either—despite all the bellows of outrage we are bound to keep hearing from worshipers of the sacred cow of Privacy.

Santa Barbara 1990

Bits and Pieces

Rhyme Scheme

Why does *stranger* rhyme with *danger?*
Why does *heart* rhyme with *apart,* and *friend* with *end?*
Why does *home* rhyme with *roam?*
And why does *nothing* rhyme with *nothing?*

San Francisco 1967

Good Show

At first I thought it was an ordinary movie. But there was something about it which seemed so real that I decided it must at least be a documentary or a newsreel. But the immediacy of the thing made me wonder if it wasn't actually being broadcast live. And then suddenly I realized that it was really happening right then and there, and that it was happening to me.

San Francisco, January 1968

Where Joys
Never Cease

Come away with me
   and we will cross continents
      on effortless wheels
         if the motor holds out

And we will fly
   through the heavens
      just a little lower than the angels
         if our passports are in order

And we will ride
   floating cities across the seas
      from nation to nation
         if we have had our shots

And we will gather
   flowers of freedom
      on the green slopes of distant mountains
         if you don't get pregnant

Orange, California 1966

Alone

And when the house was finished
You still would not live with me
You said there must be grass, there must be trees
I planted a forest
And now you cannot find your way to my door.

At Sea, October 1965

Lost

My ship went down in a sudden storm
That blew from God knows where,
With all that I prized in life aboard,
And left me drifting here.
It's not the loss of your ship that hurts,
Not most of all, I mean,
But saving not even a photograph
To prove that she wasn't a dream.

Berkeley 1964

Symbolic Suicides

1. Write your name on a piece of paper, and flush it down the toilet.

2. Put your birth certificate in a box, and bury it.

3. Put an advertisement in the paper saying that you wish to be considered dead.

4. Hang yourself in effigy.

5. Attach a photograph of yourself to a railroad track.

6 Tape an overdose of sleeping pills to the outside of your stomach.

7. March up and down with a sign saying, *I Have Killed Myself.*

San Francisco 1967

Picking a Bone

Back in the days when mothers knew best, I was taught by mine a soothing little mantra which said: "Sticks and stones may break my bones, but names can never hurt me." In the intervening 50 or so years, names nevertheless sometimes did hurt me considerably, including, ironically, a few which my mother herself chose occasionally to bestow upon me, such as "Eggs Brilliant" when I once somehow returned from a mission to the local Safeway with a dozen broken eggs. But if not all my eggs, at least all my bones managed to remain unbroken—that is, until one recent July day.

What exactly then finally fractured this long, happy record and caused me to tumble off my bicycle during an otherwise normal ride into town I will probably never know—although it could, I suppose, easily have been (lying unseen in the roadway) one of those very "sticks and stones" I had been warned about so long ago. But whatever it was, it definitely did present me, there in the middle of one of our main city streets, with a broken bone of my very own.

Never having had a broken bone before, I didn't even recognize it at the time. Even when my shoulder swelled alarmingly, I thought it must simply be a "bad sprain," since sprains were something I had experienced in the past, and could relate to. Not, in fact, until three days later, moved by the orchestrated concern of wife and personal physician, did I trouble to have some of those mysterious

X-rated photos taken of my inner self. These revealed that I actually do have the same kind of bony infrastructure as everybody else, and that, yes indeed, my clavicle (which prefers to be known as my collar-bone), was now in two slightly mis-joined pieces. The slippage was attributed to a "hairline fracture"—not very easy to see on the foggy film, but at least enough to qualify me for membership in the Broken Bone Club.

Apart from knowing that bones could be broken by sticks and stones, which was hardly of much use at this point, the only other possibly useful fact on this subject which I seem to have retained from all my years of schooling is that the collar-bone is one of those most commonly broken, and that the bones which break most easily usually heal most readily. So true has this proven in the case of my particular bone that I feel almost fraudulent in trying to get some credit for having broken it. No splint or sling was required, no special bandaging or medicine or therapy. An orthopedist, whom everybody seemed to think I had better consult, did not even suggest a second visit.

All I can honestly claim in the hope of getting any sympathy from you whatsoever is a certain amount of pain, though never enough even to keep me awake at night, and a certain amount of inconvenience, though not even enough to prevent me from writing or eating with the affected arm. On the other hand, in the weeks of recuperation, I have had the unaccustomed delight of waking every day to find myself feeling measurably improved over the day before, and able to do more and more with my injured parts. The pleasures of rapid healing have almost made me regret the approach of full recovery, when I'll simply be "normal" again.

So I've now concluded that, depending on circumstances, the question of whether breaking your bones hurts more than being called names can be something of a toss-up. (But the bones will probably still have the edge if you get tossed up hard enough.)

Santa Barbara 1988

Faith, Soap, and Charity: the Palmolive Saga

Only once in my life have I ever been able to pull off a truly brilliant public relations coup. It happened in 1966 when I was working in Orange, California, for the "Floating University" (then operating on a ship named the Ryndam), on which I also served as a teacher. Our land headquarters chanced to stand at the corner of two streets named Palm and Olive, and had thus acquired the name of Palmolive House. On the basis of that connection, I thought, wouldn't it be a great idea to contact the Palmolive Soap Company and get them interested in our school! With a list of their brand-names at hand, I wrote the following:

April 4, 1966

Dear Sirs:

HALO there! We at the Seven Seas Division of Chapman College have a true story which we believe will add LUSTRE to your name and our fame. Our office is located in a beautiful old house in Orange, California, at the corner of PALM and OLIVE Streets. Naturally, we call it PALM-OLIVE HOUSE, and naturally we have had it painted a mild and gentle Palmolive green.

131

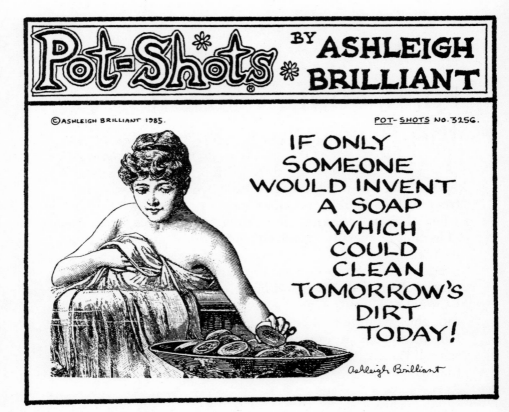

What do we do here in Palmolive House? We operate the world's only floating college campus, that's what. Sixty percent of our students are girls, and we expose that schoolgirl complexion to the balmy breezes of the tropics, the sizzling sands of the Sahara, and the salty sprays of the Seven Seas.

How would we like you to RESPOND to this news? Of course, we go WILDROOTing for ourselves. What we'd really like *you* to do is make sure that your Palmolive Soap *floats,* since otherwise it tends to damage our image as a floating campus. Failing that, instead of mere cash, your CASHMERE BOUQUET Talcum Powder, or a supply of Palmolive Soap would make a wonderful gift for our 400-coed cargo. Or, even better, a Palmolive Scholarship Fund would be a fine way of cementing, or should we say lathering, the inevitable friendship between our two great institutions.

With your cooperation, our ship might manage on its next voyage entirely to avoid the IVORY Coast.

Yours soapfully,

Ashleigh E. Brilliant
Academic Co-ordinator

Two months passed before any reply was received—and when it came, to my amazement it was in verse!—

June 3, 1966

Dear Dr. Brilliant:

We were standing here cooking our soap,
When the mailman delivered your hope-
Fully written request
To have pony expressed
Some Palmolive. We could not say "Nope."

We studied your booklet with care,
And noted the number of fair
Young ladies of learning
Who soon would be earning
Degrees *summa cum mal de mer.*

So we ordered dispatched to the hold
Of the Ryndam enough bars, all told,
To have two for each student.
The brand (we think prudent
in tropics) is Palmolive Gold. ...

So farewell, As you sail, please let us
Leave with you an idea to discuss,
Which is this: that each grade,
It cannot be gainsaid,
Earned afloat, must at least be sea-plus!

Cordially,

Arthur B. Baer, Jr.
Senior Product Manager
Colgate-Palmolive Company

The kindly corporation was as good as its word. On November 1, 1966, shortly after we sailed from New York, I had the pleasure of distributing the "golden" bars of deodorant soap in a solemn ceremony which, I like to think, nobody who was there will probably ever forget. The whole affair, a publicist's delight, culminated with my message of thanks to the Palmolive Company:

Explorers in the years of old
Crossed the seas in search of gold,
And, fearful for their limbs and lives,
Stocked their ships with guns and knives.

Today the world from shore to shore
Aboard the Ryndam we explore,
But, thanks to you, this ship of ours
Will take along its own gold bars;
And, to be safe as well as clean,
We're armed with hexachlorophene!

Beneath the Olive and the Palm
We'll venture forth without a qualm,
Free in Naples or Nigeria
From thoughtless and ill-bred bacteria.

We thank you for your noble move,
It's one the whole world should approve,
For Man still finds his brightest hope
In education—and in soap.

Companions

Old man with old dog,
Keeping each other alive.
—Who will go first?
How will the other survive?

January 1990

Angst

Am I thriving,
Or am I barely aliving?
In these times torrential,
Am I fulfilling my potential?

1977

Trust

I told the winds to blow, and they blew,
I told the birds to fly, and they flew,
I told the grass to grow, and it grew.
I also told my lover to be true.

Berkeley 1963

Preparations

I am getting ready to be lonely
I am mending fences, and putting up my walls
I am laying mines and setting traps,
And putting up signs saying
"Danger—Loneliness—Keep Out."

At Sea, October 1966

I, the Jury?

At this very moment, I am committing a criminal act. And, according to the by-now-familiar, vaguely intimidating message I have once again received from our local Superior Court, I am subjecting myself to unspecified "penalties prescribed by law." It's not what I am doing, but what I'm *not* doing, that puts me in such peril. I'm *not* telephoning a certain number, as instructed, in order to listen to a recorded message on which somebody who sounds as if she were talking in her sleep reads an incredibly long list of "panel numbers" which may or may not include mine, and thereby require me to report to the County Courthouse tomorrow at 9 A.M. for Jury Duty.

If you think I'm simply trying to avoid this vital civic responsibility, prepare yourself for another of Life's Great Ironies. The fact is that I'd like nothing better than to serve on a jury. (Well, *almost* nothing.) All my life—and certainly ever since I saw *Twelve Angry Men*—I've looked forward to having what appears to be such an interesting and potentially dramatic opportunity. When I first moved to Santa Barbara, I even called up the Jury Commissioner's office, and volunteered my services. But, despite all efforts, I have never yet been able to get onto a jury. Once I did get out of the Jury Assembly room and into an actual courtroom—but there I was soon excused on what is called a "peremptory challenge." Of course, no reason was given, but I've since been told, by people who claim to know, that "arty" or "intellectual" types never get chosen, and that

Pot-Shots BY **ASHLEIGH BRILLIANT**

© ASHLEIGH BRILLIANT 1985.

POT-SHOTS NO. 3807.

IF PLACED UNDER OATH,
I'D BE FORCED TO ADMIT
THAT
I'M NOT
REALLY
SUCH A
BAD
PERSON.

Ashleigh
Brilliant

any kind of "celebrity" status—even my own very minor-league variety—would, from a lawyer's point of view, almost certainly rule me out as a desirable juror.

It's really a pity, because I think I could do the job as well as anybody else, and I must admit it would be fun to have that much power. The right to vote as one of millions is nothing compared with the privilege of being one of just twelve sitting there and deciding somebody's fate. And if you can't be Henry Fonda holding out against eleven prejudiced people, and gradually persuading each one of them that they are wrong and that the Kid is really innocent, at least, once you get on that jury, you have the power simply to refuse to go along with all the others, and thereby single-handedly bring the whole process to a grinding halt, at enormous cost to the taxpayers.

This whole jury system is really wonderful in theory: if the dark day comes when you or I are in serious trouble with the law, we have the right to be judged ultimately by a group of ordinary citizens just like ourselves—our "peers," as the Magna Carta so quaintly puts it. But if *you're* the one in the dock, for better or worse you can be pretty sure that *I* won't be one of your peers in the jury box.

So, although I've faithfully and hopefully gone through the whole silly "jury summons" routine time after time in the past, this time I'm not even going to bother. If they really want me on a jury, they know my number, and in ten minutes by bicycle I can be at the Courthouse. Otherwise I'm prepared to face whatever the penalty is for the crime of refusing to cooperate with this absurdity. But, of course, I will first insist on a jury trial!

Santa Barbara 1988

POT-SHOTS NO. 1244.

MAKE PEACE

NOT
NOISE.

Ashleigh Brilliant © BRILLIANT ENTERPRISES 1977.

All God's Chillun
Got Earplugs

Many great things have happened in the world this year, but the greatest to me personally was my discovery of a new, improved form of ear-plug. The old kind, which I have been using for about thirty years to keep noise out of my head and some semblance of sanity in it, consisted of pieces of a wax-like substance, which always had to be softened by manipulation before they could be snugly inserted—a process which might take several seconds or minutes, depending on climatic conditions, during which time, of course, the noise, whatever it might be, was free to continue annoying.

The new kind of ear-plug, made of some kind of silicone, is in consistency more like a piece of modelling-clay or putty, always soft, and immediately ready for use. It is not (alas) significantly more sound-proof, but it does give that "fast, fast relief" which other remedial products have long boasted of in their literature.

The literature of the ear-plug itself tends to be less boastful and more cautionary, although its proud history goes back at least as far as the time of Ulysses, who, as you may remember in the *Odyssey*, stopped the ears of his crew with wax to save his ship from being lured to its doom by the song of the Sirens (a trick which, unfortunately, when it comes to stifling the shriek of today's motor-borne sirens, no brand currently on the market seems able to duplicate).

My old pre-silicone plugs came in a little blue cardboard box, containing, besides the plugs themselves (pink, cylindrical, mildly perfumed, and individually wrapped in neat little twirls of cellophane) a small sheet of instructions, which always concluded with the stern but mysterious injunction: "DO NOT CUT EAR-PLUGS!" There was never any explanation as to why anybody might even *want* to cut them, or what dire fate might befall the person who attempted to do so. Nevertheless, I played it safe, and to this day I have never cut an ear-plug, although I must confess that sheer curiosity at times made me feel mightily tempted.

While I am at it, I might as well also make another shocking confession, which is that there is something else I have never done with an ear-plug: I have never thrown one away. When they become too small to use, as somehow always happens in the course of time, I simply put them away in a drawer, where by now perhaps hundreds of them reside. I agree that the possibility of any other use ever being found for them seems small, but emotion has its place in life, and you must forgive me if I choose to be sentimental about these objects with which I have been so intimately associated for so long.

But it is more than mere romantic attachment which has endeared my ear-plugs to me. They also symbolize some of the finest aspects of our civilization. The ear-plug user is in many cases a person who voluntarily undergoes a degree of inconvenience and self-sacrifice in order to secure relief which might otherwise be obtained only by calculated acts of violence and destruction.

In a world where those who produce noise still seem so completely to have the upper hand over those who suffer from its effects (just as smokers prevailed over non-smokers barely a generation ago), where, even in a community so relatively enlightened as my own, one person with a machine which does nothing but blow dirt can still have the legal right to disturb the peace of hundreds of others in the vicinity, ear-plugs must be accorded their own very special place of honor.

I myself have fought some incredibly valiant battles

against intrusive noises of the kind which overwhelm all attempts to plug them out. There was one episode in London, in 1972, which involved my making night-time "commando" raids against a powerful compressor, which in the daytime was turning my dwelling, outside which it had established itself, into a hell-on-earth. Unfortunately I did not have the technical knowledge to dis-voice the beast, and for some reason the sugar I poured into its fuel-tank did nothing either to silence or sweeten it. Finally I tried a desperate plea to the local Public Health authorities, and, to my surprise, this actually worked, at least to the extent of their requiring that a sound-suppressing wooden covering be placed over the machine.

That noise of all kinds can be a genuine health hazard is scarcely open any longer to serious scientific debate. But only too often such appeals to reason (especially when one is confronting the owner of an obstreperous dog or a fearsome snore) fall, so to speak, upon deaf ears. Just how great the need for self-deafening has become since the days when the little blue box was the only game in town is evident when I go into any large drug-store today and see how many different types and brands of ear-plugs are now available. Yet none can give total protection, and each competing brand is required by the U.S. Environmental Protection Agency to state, in very technical terms, exactly how many decibels of relief it is supposed to provide.

But to me what will ultimately always appeal most about ear-plugs is not their *science,* but their *poetry.* It is my hope one day to found an anti-noise organization whose acronym will be that most beautiful of words: H.U.S.H.—for *H*umans *U*nderstanding *S*ound and *H*earing. And its anthem will be my own version of a plaintive old spiritual:

I got ear-plugs, you got ear-plugs,
All God's chillun got ear-plugs—
When I get to Heaven, gonna take out my ear-plugs,
Gonna listen all over God's Heaven.

Santa Barbara 1989

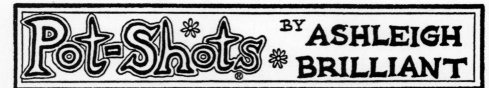
Pot-Shots BY ASHLEIGH BRILLIANT

SOMEDAY I'LL GET
MY BIG CHANCE—

OR HAVE I
ALREADY HAD IT?

Ashleigh
Brilliant

Going Bananas

Have you ever dreamed of winning instant fame in some big contest, and receiving one of those exciting Grand Prizes which promise to whisk you away from wherever you are and deposit you in some romantic location amid all-expense-paid luxury and splendor? The closest I ever came to such bliss was in 1986. My memories of the experience are tinged with sadness, but the tale must be told.

Rarely do I enter contests of any kind, because my chances of winning usually seem discouragingly small. But one day in May 1986, when I came upon a pad of entry forms in my local supermarket announcing a contest to write new lyrics to the Chiquita Banana Song, a surge of excitement went through me. Writing words to existing melodies happens to be one of the few things I am pretty good at—and in this case, the song, which must be one of the most enduring of all commercial jingles, was one I had known and loved ever since I first heard it on the radio as a child in the 1940's:

> I'm Chiquita Banana, and I've come to say
> Bananas like to ripen in a certain way—
> When they are flecked with brown and have a golden hue,
> Bananas taste the best, and are the best for you.
> You can put them in a salad,
> You can put them in a pie—aye!
> Any way you like to eat them
> It's impossible to beat them.
> But bananas like the climate of the
> very very tropical equator,
> So you should never put bananas
> In your refrigerator.
> No no no no, La la la.   ©United Brands Company

That little song, with its charming Latin lilt, had been part of my cultural heritage for forty years. In fact, I had already published one "new version" of it in 1967, in my *Haight-Ashbury Songbook,* which celebrated the San Francisco "Hippie Scene"—using it to satirize the then-current rumor (alas, soon discredited) that bananas could actually be smoked, to produce a psychedelic—and legal—"high":

> I'm Chiquita Banana, here to testify
> Bananas are so good, and they can get you high!
> So for discreet and law-abiding gentlefolk,
> There's nothing like the fragrance of banana smoke.
> It can bring you to Nirvana,
> But they can't ban a banana;
> You can stock it and retail it,
> And its even safe to mail it!
> So if there's no other reason but the law that
> has been keeping you angelic,
> Remember beautiful bananas
> Can make you psychedelic!
> They can't ban a ba-na-na!

This contest, then, seemed a natural for me, and my chances, for once, appeared very good, especially since not one, but *ten* identical "Grand Prizes" were being offered. The prize itself, however, was in this case hardly grand enough to provide any kind of extraordinary motivation. It was not a cruise to the tropics, or even a lifetime supply of bananas. It was merely a luxury weekend for two in Los Angeles.

Los Angeles happens to be practically next-door to Santa Barbara, where I live. And many of my fellow Santa Barbarans would consider a compulsory weekend there, no matter how luxurious, as a penalty rather than a prize. Even to Dorothy and me, with our slightly more tolerant standards, the prospect was hardly the thrill of a lifetime. The package would indeed include two nights in a fancy hotel, two breakfasts and two dinners in posh places, plus one evening's entertainment in a "comedy club," and limousine transportation throughout. And it was stated to have a total retail value of $2000. But you couldn't settle for the cash, or even transfer the prize to somebody else. You had to take the luxury weekend or nothing, and you had to take it between October 10 and December 21, 1986.

But all that, in this case, hardly mattered to me. What really mattered was the chance, as I saw it, of winning eternal glory as a lyricist. Nowhere in the information supplied did it actually say what use if any would be made of the winning entries. But the whole promotion did call itself a "Sing Your Way to the Top" contest, and I had ecstatic dreams of becoming famous as the Man Who Wrote the New Improved Chiquita Banana Song. Maybe they wouldn't actually use my voice on the new commercial which I presumed they were planning, but surely there would be some kind of spectacular ceremony in which I would be publicly introduced (perhaps wearing a banana costume), and given a chance to sing my new classic for the microphones and cameras of a waiting world. And for years, possibly generations, to come, it would be *my* words which in the minds of millions would become synonymous with bananas. It was this rapturous vision which now propelled me into a frenzy of creative activity.

The Great Banana Contest, 1986.

CHIQUITA is a registered trademark of United Brands Company, 1986.

There was also, I must admit, the sheer *challenge* of the task. However great my own talents, there was bound to be tremendous competition. Every song-writer in the country, every poet, every banana-lover, would be eyeing *this* prize. Whatever I sent in would have to be absolutely unbeatable. But what did the judges really *want?* What were they looking for? I read the rules over and over. The only stated requirement was that the new song "must be about Chiquita bananas," and must begin with that same familiar first line, "I'm Chiquita Banana, and I've come to say..." Entries would be judged on the basis of "originality," "lyric writing ability," and "appropriateness to Chiquita image, character, and product."

I could only conclude that what they wanted was something clever, cute, and informative, which would also sell bananas. The rest was up to me. There were many different possible approaches, but fortunately there was no limit on how many times I could enter. Armed to the hilt with all the banana facts I could muster, I launched myself into the banana song business in a big way, and for the next several weeks it absorbed me totally.

By the deadline date of August 6, I had sent in a whole bunch of banana songs—a dozen completely different versions, each one of which I felt was good enough to be picked. In all modesty, I must say that I consider this act of mass creation one of the great achievements of my life. But don't take my word for it. At the risk of driving you bananas, too, I will exhibit here the entire collection:

(1)

I'm Chiquita Banana, and I've come to say:
Nutritionally speaking, I am quite OK.
High in Potassium, but low in fat content,
I'm rich in carbohydrate (twenty-two percent).
You can nourish with a flourish—
Vitamins both C and A—yay!
Be robuster and add luster
To your table with a cluster.
I'm right here through all the year, you never have to
wait for me until mañana.
The general feeling's I'm a-peeling,
So have a nice banana!
You really should (they're so good!)

(2)

I'm Chiquita Banana, and I've come to say:
No other fruit can ever rival my display.
I go from green to gold, as you will soon observe—
An easy-open package with a lovely curve.
My nutrition's elevated,
But my price is never sky-high.
As you see my surface brightening,
You will know that I am ripening.
Let the color get no duller than a faintly
speckled gold on my complexion.
Then you can savor all my flavor,
And you will taste perfection!
Go go go go Ba-na-nas!

(3)

I'm Chiquita Banana, and I've come to say:
Bananas have the energy to make your day.
They're luscious mashed or firm, they're lovely fresh or dried,
So many tasty ways of pleasing your inside!
You can slice them into ice-cream,
They can bake or they can fry-aye!
You can blend them into juices,
Every mealtime they have uses.
So if you're in search of ways to make your
days and menus healthier and sweeter,
Just let your plans include bananas,
And make them all Chiquita!
For every wish I'm your dish!

(4)

I'm Chiquita Banana, and I've come to say:
Please don't misunderstand me, it is quite OK
To put me in your fridge, but only when I'm ripe—
Till then the climate I prefer is tropical type.
You will love my carbohydrate,
And I've no cholester—olé.
Every way bananas taste fine,
And they won't expand your waistline!
Any season there's good reason for bananas in
your plans and on your table.
The place to meet a sweet Chiquita
Is where you see my label.
Go go go go ba-na-nas!

(5)

I'm Chiquita Banana, and I've come to say:
A bountiful banana goes with work or play.
For a nutritious snack, and for a tasty treat—
So easily prepared, so very good to eat.
Lunch or dinner, I'm a winner,
Any meal you want to try-aye,
From your breakfast to your supper,
I'm a wholesome picker-upper.
With potassium and vitamins, I'm good for health
as well as for your pleasure.
What's there for you in a banana?
—A truly golden treasure!
Your food of fun (from the sun)!

149

(6)

I'm Chiquita Banana, and I've come to say:
For health and fun, bananas are the natural way.
We have no additives, no empty calories,
We come designed for you from Nature's galleries.
We can fit into your diet,
You'll find many ways to try it.
Young and old are interested,
We're so easily digested.
So if flavorsome nutrition with good value is
what you are seeking, then you
Should keep Chiquita's fine bananas
In mind and on your menu!
Keep us in sight (we're so right)!

(7)

I'm Chiquita Banana, and I've come to say:
More people choose bananas round the world today.
Such a nutritious food you love from babyhood—
So easily digested, and they taste so good!
They're superb in pies or caking,
Also other things you're making.
You can slice or you can squash them,
You don't even have to wash them!
For convenience and economy and health and
pleasure, nothing could be plainer—
Bananas bring you what I sing you
In such a cute container!
Delicious deal (and appeal)!

(8)

I'm Chiquita Banana, and I've come to say:
Bananas have a bonus for you every day.
Not only smooth and sweet and just a joy to eat—
Bananas give you nourishment from head to feet!
Yes, my contents are not nonsense:
Vitamins and miner-olé!
In whatever form you try, you
Will find they really satisfy you.
In a cake or salad, pie or fritters its so
true, banana goodness lingers—
But nothing beats a ripe banana
You peel with your own fingers!
No nothing beats BA-NA-NAS!

(9)

I'm Chiquita Banana, and I've come to say:
Bananas are so popular, they're here to stay.
No matter what the time, the season or the date,
Some nourishing bananas should be on your plate.
As a pudding or a filling,
You will find them most a-peeling.
From your oven or your blender,
They can help to keep you slender.
And it's much more than the flavor that makes
people choose bananas by a wide rate—
It's vitamins and miner-olé
And lots of carbohydrate!
A food ideal any meal!

(10)

> I'm Chiquita Banana, and I've come to say:
> Where there's a ripe banana, there's a happy way
> To get a lift that's healthy, full of flavor too—
> Enjoy yourself and do yourself a favor too.
> Keep bananas in your kitchen,
> There are vitamins they're rich in.
> With your meals or when you're snacking
> Is when bananas are lip-smacking.
> But it really doesn't matter what the season or the
> reason or your plan is—
> It's always good taste and good manners
> When people go bananas!
> Go go go go ba-na-nas!

(11)

> I'm Chiquita Banana, and I've come to say:
> At home or work or school, or even on your way,
> Bananas bring the best to you for health and fun—
> Good taste and good nutrition from the tropical sun.
> Life, no matter what your plan is
> Can be better with bananas.
> In the morning or the night time
> For bananas is the right time.
> But it's dangerous and unsightly to be careless
> with the peel of a banana,
> So my proposal is disposal
> In an appropriate manner.
> Go go go go ba-na-nas!

(12)

> I'm Chiquita Banana, and I've come to say:
> If you really love bananas, you should work and pray
> For peace and friendship every place beneath the sky—
> (You cannot grow bananas where the bullets fly!)
> But it's hard to go on fighting
> While bananas you are biting.
> Brotherhood: let's realize it,
> Let bananas symbolize it!
> So it's time to make bananas what they ought to be
> by all my observations:
> Official fruit for good relations
> Of the United Nations!
> Make trouble cease: munch in peace.

As you will see, in most versions I tried to retain the spirit of the original ditty. My researches had revealed, however, (somewhat to my horror) that the old song's stern injunction against refrigerating bananas under any circumstances had been misleading, and I boldly revised this article of faith in No. 4. But only in No. 12, mindful of turbulence in certain banana-growing regions of the world, did I yield to the temptation to write a less commercial and more idealistic type of "message."

Having made such prodigious efforts, I naturally awaited the contest results with pathetic eagerness. And on September 12, 1986, the word came. I was indeed a winner!

It is here, however, that my banana story begins to turn from gold to a darker and more somber shade. For it was at this point that I expected the portals of banana heaven to open before me. But nothing happened. Of course I would now be entitled to that "fabulous" weekend in Los Angeles. But what I wanted was some direct acknowledgement of my achievement from the Chiquita Company—some word of admiration and appreciation, some indication of how they would use the set of masterpieces I had produced for them. You may think I was hopelessly naive. But somehow I had been so caught up in the agonies and ecstasies of creation that the banal realities of my "success" came as a series of unpleasant surprises.

The first surprise was that I never heard directly from the Chiquita Banana Company at all—and indeed have never heard from them to this day. The letter announcing my triumph came from a New York firm called Marden-Kane, which had been hired to administer and judge the contest, and which obviously had no more interest in bananas than they had in me as an individual. The letter did little more than repeat the carefully itemized description of the prize weekend as stated in the contest rules, and ask me to choose when I wanted to have it. There was not a word about my incredible performance as a banana bard, and not even any indication as to which of my 12 entries had been the winner, let alone any details about what was going to be done with any of them. And these people had the nerve to conclude their letter by congratulating me on my "good fortune"—as if my name had simply been drawn out of a barrel!

Desperate for more recognition than this, I telephoned Marden-Kane, and managed to establish that the chosen version had been my No. 11. But they could tell me nothing else, except that "my" contest had not been nation-wide in scope, but was only one of many similar ones held in different regions at different times. This of course was another let-down.

I could only hope that the prize weekend itself, which Dorothy and I fixed for November 28-30, would somehow make amends for this deflation. Surely at the hotel or the night-club or one of the restaurants, special arrangements would have been made, and I would at least be acknowledged as a Chiquita Banana winner and asked to perform my winning song. But even that modest dream went up in banana smoke. Yes, there was a limousine; yes, there was an elegant suite in Westwood; yes, there were opulent meals and entertainment; but yes, there was no banana song ever called for anywhere. The other nine winners had apparently all chosen other weekends, so we didn't meet any of them. Nobody cared about why we were there. At each place, we simply presented a voucher, and were treated like ordinary customers.

On Sunday afternoon, November 30, the limousine took us home to Santa Barbara, still wearing our weekend finery. As we drove back up State Street, I stood up and looked out of the sun-roof, and waved to the few people I saw. Nobody knew who I was or what I had done to be deserving this honor. People shouted "Who are you?," "What are you running for?" One even called "Heil Hitler!" I was weary with worn-out hope, and didn't even have the heart to respond with a banana song.

The rest of the story is scarcely any more uplifting. In an effort to find out more about the fate of my lyrics, I wrote to a New York "promotion company" called Cato Johnson, apparently also in the employ of Chiquita Banana, to whom Marden-Kane had shunted me off—but no reply ever came. Hoping at least to compare notes with others in my position, I wrote to another address, as instructed in the contest rules, for a list of the winners, but never received one.* And, as a crowning humiliation, although the rules also stated that "winning entrants will be required to execute all necessary documents to transfer any right, title

In a luxurious hotel, the Incredible Banana Bard enjoys the fruits,
so to speak, of his great achievement. But no bananas!

or interest in the lyrics they have written for their entry" no such documents were ever even presented to me. Obviously, Chiquita Banana had no interest whatsoever in the magnificent tribute I had laid upon her altar.

If this were a better world, I suppose I would not still be suffering from this lingering case of sour bananas. I would forget all about the contest, and simply go back to enjoying bananas for their own sake, as I used to. But the truth is that for many years—in fact, since long before the contest—I haven't even been able to eat bananas. For some reason, they just don't agree with me any more.

Santa Barbara 1990

*Four years later, while preparing this account, I sent again to Marden-Kane, by certified mail, a polite request for the list of winners, and was not even honored with an acknowledgment.

Ashleigh Brilliant

POT-SHOTS NO. 624

CONGRATULATE ME!

*I don't
love you
any more!*

Here is another song from my Haight-Ashbury Songbook, a tabloid sold on the streets of San Francisco during the famous 1967 "Summer of Love." This ballad had very personal meaning for me, but also reflected what seemed at that time to be a general youthful turning away from academia. The Hippie culture was then flowering in the Haight-Ashbury, a district in the heart of San Francisco, while on the other side of San Francisco Bay, Berkeley, home of the University of California, had recently been convulsed by a "Free Speech Movement."

The Girl I Left in Berkeley

(To the tune of "The Girl I Left Behind Me.")

Oh I've left girls in many a town,
from here to Albuquerque,
But there's just one who let *me* down—
The girl I left in Berkeley.
She knew the pain I'd feel to leave,
And didn't want to hurt me,
So, before I left her, she left me—
The girl I left in Berkeley.

We knew our Constitutional rights,
And sought to guarantee them,
And so at school we joined the fight
For Academic Freedom.
We loved Free Speech and spoke Free Love,
but I didn't mean it really—
Although it's fair to love and share,
Some share their love too freely.

So in despair, I left her there,
And, vowing I'd be wary,
I crossed the Bay one fateful day,
And came to Haight Ashbury.

157

I looked around until I found
A girl with looks and knowledge,
And she taught me that, to be free,
You don't need books or college.

Oh school is just a big machine,
And college girls can leave you—
It's better on the Hippie scene—
A Hippie won't deceive you.
Oh I've left girls regretfully,
From Mexico to Turkey—
But I'm not so sad that she left me—
The girl I left in Berkeley.

San Francisco 1967

Resignation

It isn't good, it isn't right
But I will sleep alone tonight;
But I will sleep, and then go on
As if I had not slept alone.
The sun will circle into view
As bright as if my bed held two,
And I will eat and breathe and read
As if I had no other need.
It isn't bad, it isn't wrong—
Each way the night is just as long.

Berkeley 1963

See Your
Travail Agent

It is now a whole generation since a couple of non-super men in funny suits first took up a very temporary residence on the surface of the Moon. They said they did it for all of us, and most of us believed that we would soon be following them. Scores of thousands of hopeful Americans, in fact, soon applied to Pan-Am for reservations to be on the first commercial flight to the Moon. My wife and I, who were among them, still have the official acknowledgement of our request, and are presumably still on the waiting-list. But now Pan-Am is in the process of going bankrupt, and that list (according to a recent news report) languishes in some vault on an old computer tape, its fate as unsettled as that of the entire space program. It looks as if we will have to wait some time longer before putting on our Moon shoes.

In the meantime, for better or worse, we are all trapped here on Earth, a planet which, as everyone knows, is becoming increasingly overcrowded, over-used, and subject to the disease of creeping sameness. It is a world where (with the necessary funds) you can now get with almost ridiculous ease from any place to anywhere else. When you arrive, you can live in climate-controlled comfort and enjoy the same kind of food, facilities, and conveniences you had at home. On the other hand, if you stay put, you can, thanks to modern trade and technology, buy most of the

POT-SHOTS NO. 1377.

I HAVE
TRAVELLED WIDELY,
AND HAVE
LEARNED TO
COUGH AND SNEEZE

IN MANY DIFFERENT LANGUAGES.

© ASHLEIGH BRILLIANT 1978

same goods, eat the same foods, and even experience the same sights and sounds as if you were far away. And, no matter where you happen to be at the moment, you can communicate almost instantaneously with just about any other point on the globe.

In such a world as this, the question naturally arises, why travel at all any more? Those involved in what is called the Travel Industry will answer with market-tested words like Escape, Romance, and Adventure. But we know they are lying. I have my own answer. You won't like it, but it is the truth: the only remaining legitimate reason for traveling is to *suffer*—to endure various kinds of stress, difficulty, and pain which you don't normally get by staying at home. And, if you return from a trip with no horror stories, having had nothing but pleasure, smooth sailing, and no surprises, you can perhaps qualify as a very successful tourist—but you haven't really *traveled* at all.

The very world "travel" in fact comes directly from the word "travail," which combines the ideas of labor and of suffering. Until comparatively recent times, it was taken for granted that a journey of any consequence would necessarily involve considerable effort and risk. People routinely made their wills before setting out on ocean voyages. Pilgrimages were undertaken to distant holy places because the very act of enduring a long journey was a kind of sacrifice and a demonstration of faith. It is easy to forget all that, in these days of package tours, when we ourselves have become the packages, being shipped in insulated containers from one safely sanitized "attraction" to another.

So, if you do happen to get sick, robbed, lost, or stuck on your next trip, you must not think of it a some kind of flaw or defect in your total travel experience, but rather as an essential part of it. Travel, in order to have any meaning for ours, the last earth-bound generations, must be seen as a metaphor of our whole existence. The ravages of insect pests, the curse of jet-lag, the hazards of terrorist attacks, the arrogance of petty officials, the smells of primitive toilets, the fear and agony of simply not understanding what is going on—"these" you must say to yourself, "These are what I came for."

My wife unfortunately does not see things this way. Unlike me, she is a born tourist—a word which significantly derives from the idea of a *turning*, or *circular*, journey. The tourist, unlike the traveler, confidently expects to return, and to do so in a certain way at a certain time. A tour can be planned, and much of its activity tends to center around thoughts of being home again—as in the purchase of souvenirs and the taking of photographs—trophies, as it were, to display as proofs of one's pseudo-exploits. The real traveler, of course, needs no such verification of his experiences, since he usually has actual scars.

My wife loves luxurious hotels, large airports, elegant restaurants, banks, department stores—all the milieus which I as a traveler disdain. My travel-haunts are the police stations, the lost-property offices, the hospital emergency rooms. I seem to make a hobby of being sick in various countries. For this reason I prefer surface transportation. Instead of going as fast as possible, I would rather linger with one illness than hurry on to the next. My peak of excruciation was perhaps reached on a long ocean voyage from England to Australia on which, while prostrated with what was later diagnosed as pneumonia, I was exposed for hours on end to the non-stop shrieking of a child in the adjoining cabin, whose parents, despite my pitiful protests, insisted on their right to keep her locked alone there while they were enjoying themselves on deck.

If such delights do not appeal to you, I do have one other answer to the travel problem. A new frontier is opening up, full of excitement and promise. It is called *home*. I envisage the rise of a new professional: the Non-Travel Agent, who will arrange activities for us in our own communities. Instead of Bon Voyage parties, there will be *non*-voyage parties, where we will celebrate our avoidance of expensive, time-consuming, exhausting foreign forays. In time, with the advance of technology, we will be able to send out increasingly sophisticated robots, to do for us whatever in the way of Earth travel still seems worth doing.

In the meantime, however, being married to a tourist, I can't entirely escape the consequences of her susceptibility to the allure of the brochure, even though I try to get to the mail first and discard the more outrageous ones. Of course, she respects my feelings about the value of suffering—once she actually hitch-hiked with me for several days in Europe, an experience miserable enough to fulfill all my requirements. Usually, however, we compromise, and do things her way. And when that trip to the Moon finally comes off, I have every expectation of being totally Moon-sick before she has even half-finished buying all her Moon T-shirts and Moon mugs.

Santa Barbara 1991

POT-SHOTS NO. 1233

THE REPORTS ON
HUMAN PROGRESS
ARE BEGINNING
TO COME IN,

AND SOME ARE
A LITTLE
DISCOURAGING.

Ashleigh Brilliant

String 'em Down!

Imagine an eyesore so monstrous that, instead of existing in just one spot, it reaches out over a whole town, defacing streets, obstructing views, and casting a pall of ugliness over houses, trees, and sky. Regardless of where you live, the chances are that you don't have to imagine it. We are all victims of the ghastly blight of utility poles and wires which seems to have settled itself upon us forever.

Incredibly, for more than a century we have tolerated this flimsy plague of wood and wire, which was obviously erected in great haste, and without the slightest consideration of aesthetic values. Look at photographs taken a hundred years ago, and you will see that everything else has changed since then—the architecture, the vehicles, the styles of dress—but one thing is hideously familiar: those ugly poles, draped with all their crossbars and wires, have hardly changed at all. And all the time, the whole system could have been put where our sewers and gas-pipes already naturally are: *underground!*

True, this is at least one problem which is not getting worse. In areas of new development, all utility lines are often required to be underground. And many wire-ridden communities have in theory some long-term scheme for gradually burying all the existing overhead lines. But the cost is very high, and priority is usually given to business districts—and even there, progress is so slow that plans seldom even exist for relieving the residential streets. Unless we do something about it, this grotesque form of visual pollution may prevail for the rest of our lives.

Yet, this is not as simple a problem as it ought to be. Many people, I know, have become so habituated to this particular species of ugliness that they take it almost as part of the natural order of things. And there are probably some who actually *like* poles and wires, and who will form societies to fight their removal, so that birds will still have somewhere to congregate and cars will still have something to crash into. Many others (possibly, I fear, the majority), will be all in favor of the massive job of putting everything underground, but will not be willing to pay anything towards it. And, no doubt, some will argue that, with so many more pressing problems in the world, and having lived in the shadow of this one all our lives, we can easily bequeath it to our children.

Mine may indeed be a voice crying in the wirey wilderness, so long as I continue to dwell upon aesthetic considerations. Beauty, it seems, is not enough. In order to get any action, I may have to join the anguished chorus of those who suspect that our physical health is also at risk from the multitude of electric currents seething overhead and all around us. But, one way or another, we must make it a priority project to remove this gigantic blemish from the face of our land. To put it poetically,

> I think I never shall admire
> A line of poles festooned with wire,
> And hope someday they'll all be found
> (Before I get there) *underground.*

Santa Barbara 1988

Two Sonnets

I don't write sonnets unless I have to—and there have been only two occasions in my life when I had to. The first was when assigned to do so for a college English class. I was a graduate student living meagerly on scholarship, so I took the opportunity to celebrate my poverty in immortal verse:

A Sonnet on Sardines

Ten cents a day is all I can afford
For lunch, and so sardines I then devour—
One little can at noontime, my reward
For living through the morning till that hour.
With desk half-cleared, and papers pushed aside,
With can and implements before me neatly spread,
I set to work, and, with a certain pride
Of craftsmanship, exhume the fishy dead.
Unseemly haste must not deprave my feast,
I cherish every morsel as a boon
Which, by affection bounteously increased,
Sustains my spirits through the afternoon.
Ah, call me riff-raff, ruffian, rascal, rude—
But never say I have no love for food!

Claremont, California 1957

My second sonnet somehow arose many years later, not from external but from internal compulsion, while reading Walter Jackson Bate's fine biography of Keats.

Going On

I hear no call—no purpose seeks me out,
No light shines down on my appointed task,
No instinct overcomes all sense of doubt,
No answers quench the questions I must ask.
To do or not to do seems all the same—
Whatever's writ, by Time must be erased—
To build a home, an empire, or a name
Must equally in the long run be a waste.
And yet, and yet, some power drives me on,
Some dream from which I've not yet come awake
Persuades me that, before this dream is gone,
There is some part of it I have to make.
I'll never know for sure which way is right,
But there are many pathways through the night.

Santa Barbara 1986

The War Memoirs
of Ashleigh Brilliant

Hitler didn't invade Poland until September, but, in my memory, the war begins with a song which I must have heard people singing in London sometime early in 1939:

Underneath the spreading chestnut tree,
There Mr. Chamberlain said to me
"If you want to get your gas-mask free,
Join the blinking A.R.P.!"

I was five years old. The song was rather puzzling to me, but I soon learned that "A.R.P." meant "Air Raid Precautions." And I saw men doing some strange digging in the park across the street from our house. And I somehow acquired my own gas-mask, with an unforgettable rubbery smell when you put it on. That, as things turned out, was as close as I ever came to direct involvement in the war as a little English boy.

In April 1939, in what was still officially peacetime, my mother took me and my sister (who was just three) on a trip, supposed to be for a few months, across the Atlantic, to visit our relations in my mother's home town of Toronto, Canada. We sailed on the *Ascania*, not knowing that we wouldn't see England again for seven long years.

The outbreak of war meant that we could not return home, but had to go on living in Toronto, in a series of

POT-SHOTS NO. 3361.

SO MANY
OF US
ARE
PRODUCTS
OF A
BROKEN
WORLD.

Ashleigh
Brilliant

apartments and rented rooms, while my father, a British Civil Servant, remained back in England, and endured the bombing, which we experienced only in the newsreels. (I remember the chorus of sympathetic sighs from the Canadian movie audience, at pictures of injured British children being rescued from bombed houses.) Our own house was never hit, but we lost it anyway. It was "requisitioned" by the British government to house other people, and even after the war we were never able to get it back again. (It still stands, and I still have fantasies that someday I may buy it, and somehow recover the happiness of my lost English childhood).

Then, in the spring of 1941, we learned that my father had managed to get transferred to Washington, D.C. For anxious weeks, we knew he was coming over, but had no idea exactly how or when. Finally, one day in June, when the three of us were in our small apartment on College Street, the telephone rang, and it was my father! He was in Halifax, Nova Scotia. The freighter on which he was a passenger had been torpedoed and sunk by a German submarine, and he had barely escaped with his life.

Several days later, he reached Toronto. After more than two years, I hardly knew this man with the moustache and glasses and strange English accent. He had a frightening story to tell, about dangling at the end of a rope ladder on the side of a sinking ship, with only the waves beneath him. But what most impressed me were the English coins he showed us. They had been in his pocket when he left the ship, and the water of the sea had stained them green.

But now, at last, we were all together again, and soon we were living in another apartment, this time in Washington, D.C., where my father's job somehow meant that my sister and I were no longer "evacuees," but had become "diplomat's children." As in Toronto, we went to the ordinary public schools, and our friends were the neighborhood kids. But we always knew that, when the war was over, we would be going back home to an England which, in the meantime, however, sank into ever more distant memory.

In that summer of 1941, moving from Canada to the U.S. meant going from a country at war to one not officially at war yet. But I was hardly conscious of this subtle distinction. In any case, everything was changed in December by an attack on a place I had never heard of before: Pearl Harbor. It was hard for me to understand what Hawaii and Japan had to do with the old familiar war against Hitler and the Germans. But, once again, a song (which we learned at school just a short time after the event) helped to put it all in focus for me, especially the lines at the end:

> We will always remember
> How they died for Liberty;
> Let's remember Pearl Harbor,
> And go on to Vic-tor-y!

Somehow the idea that those people had "died for liberty" was quite novel to me. Until then, I had thought that the only real issue in the war was the question of when my family would be able to go home. Now, as I reached the age of eight, the whole conflict seemed to acquire new meaning.

As a child growing up in wartime America, especially in the city known as "Our Nation's Capital" I took the war very seriously and very patriotically. Naturally, I felt a particular interest in the British role, and this was reinforced by various British Government publications, designed to strengthen Anglo-American relations, which my father brought home from his office. But America's war was my war too.

Of course, we were all involved in what was called the "War Effort." There was Rationing—a sort of game played with paper coupons, and later with plastic tokens. (Gasoline rationing, however, never affected my family, because we never had a car.) There were air-raid drills at school, in which, for some reason, we all had to go and sit in the corridors. Our toys were very much war-oriented. (I had a board game called "Spot-a-Plane" in which winning depended upon correctly identifying various war-planes from their silhouettes.) We bought "war savings stamps" at school, which we stuck in special little books. And we helped with "scrap drives" by saving tin cans. (I enjoyed stamping them flat after taking off the ends.) You couldn't go down any street without being reminded of the war, and all the people who were away in it, because of all the houses that had little banners in their windows with a certain number of blue (or sometimes, sadly, gold) stars.

But for me it was a war fought mostly on the radio, in the movies, and in comic-books. I never questioned our side's total rightness, or the enemy's total wrongness. I knew that we had to demand unconditional surrender— especially after I heard a radio play in which one of the characters said so (although my mother taught me a new word when she dismissed that part of the script as "propaganda"). And I knew that one day we, the Allies, would invade both Germany and Japan, and bring all their leaders to justice in some big trial.

There was one other thing I knew as an article of faith, and it calls to mind the most shocking thing I ever heard my mother say. One day I asked her quite innocently "Mummy, what will they do with all the guns when the war is over?" and she said, "I suppose they'll save them for the next war." To me, this was blasphemy. Every child in America knew, from everything we read and heard, that there wouldn't, mustn't, couldn't ever be another war— that this war was being fought for our sake, so that we, the children, would be able to grow up and live our lives in a world free from war.

As time went on, I followed the war news with increasing awareness. By the late spring of 1944 I knew, as did everybody else, that the big invasion of Europe was imminent. It would begin on what had already been dubbed D-Day. I remember speculating about the exact date with my best friend Nathan, and saying, "Wouldn't it be funny if D-day came on my father's birthday!" (which was June 4). My prediction turned out to be just two days early.

The final year of the war is much more vivid in my mind than all the preceding ones. But for me it was full of disappointments and bewilderments. The big invasion did not lead to the immediate downfall of Hitler, and even by Christmas of 1944 there was still much fighting going on in an area called the "Belgian Bulge." In fact, as was proudly announced in one of our school assemblies at Paul Junior High School, one hero of that battle was a brother of Miss McAuliffe, our assistant principal. (It was General Anthony McAuliffe, who made the famous one-word reply to a German demand for the surrender of his troops trapped at Bastogne: *Nuts!*)

I was 11 when the end finally did come in 1945, and another let-down was that by then many of the war's chief figures, who had been part of my world ever since I could remember, had already left the scene. First President Roosevelt died (a blow which I felt most keenly in the discontinuation for several days of many of my favorite radio programs). Then, within a few weeks, Hitler, Mussolini, Goebbels, and Himmler were also dead—all without ever being "brought to justice" at the big trial I had always looked forward to. And Germany had scarcely surrendered when Prime Minister Churchill, the very soul of our war effort, was incredibly voted out of office by the people of Britain. How could this happen?

The joy of victory was also spoiled by what were called the "Nazi Atrocities," of which we now began to become aware for the first time, with special free public showings of "atrocity films," which my parents went to, and told us about grimly, but which children were not even allowed to see.

But still, Europe was "liberated," and I expressed my own feelings in a poem I called "We Shall Remember":

> *When this war's graves are counted*
> *And we see the cost,*
> *We should look up to Heaven*
> *And thank God that we hadn't lost....*

And if we forget those fighters brave,
And how the whole world they did save,
It will not be worth trying to save it again,
If we do not remember those men.

However, there was still the Pacific War, in which our forces had been steadily advancing towards the "home islands" of Japan. Here at least things seemed to be going as they were supposed to. General MacArthur really did return to the Philippines, just as he had said he would. Surely this would all climax with another big invasion.

But then came a totally unexpected development called The Atomic Bomb. It seemed completely out of scale with the rest of the war, and almost unnecessary. Why hadn't it come in time to use against Hitler? Now, all it meant was that there would be no invasion of Japan after all. Even more perplexing, when Japan did surrender, Hirohito, whom I had always been taught to regard as a chief villain and major war criminal, was amazingly allowed to stay on as Emperor—an outcome with which, over the remaining 40 years of his reign, I was never totally at ease.

Nevertheless, the war's end did have the one result which I had always most hoped for—my family did go "home" again. But, after years of comparative comfort and plenty in the U.S., we found England bleak and impoverished. My sister and I never managed to re-establish our roots there; and eventually all four of us came back to America.

In one sense, I have always felt glad to have had the war in my childhood, because, as a result, nothing that has happened in the world since then has ever seemed quite so bad. On the other hand, I never entirely got over my feeling of being cheated when the promised era of peace in a wonderful "post-war world" failed to materialize. I could not understand how, after *all that*, people could ever even think of fighting again. And I still can't.

Santa Barbara 1990

175

Pot-Shots BY ASHLEIGH BRILLIANT

POT-SHOTS NO. 3883.

I HAVE MANY
UNRECOGNIZED
TALENTS ~

BUT MY FAULTS
HAVE SOMEHOW
SUCCEEDED
IN SECURING
WIDE RECOGNITION.

Ashleigh Brilliant

Nothing to Sneeze at

For most of my life I thought I was the only one in the world who could do it. I certainly never saw anyone else doing it, and nothing I ever read or heard even mentioned it. It was a gift, a little secret I had with myself. The secret lay in a mysterious connection I had discovered sometime in my childhood between bright light and sneezing. When I wanted to sneeze, I could look at the sun, or whatever other light was available, and thereby somehow help myself to bring it on. It has always worked for me, and, even when I don't want to sneeze, coming suddenly from a relatively dark place into bright sunlight can often cause me to have one, two, or three sneezes (but, rather mysteriously, never more than three).

My wife simply couldn't understand it. She would watch in bewilderment as I might suddenly, in the middle of a conversation, become fascinated by a light bulb in which I had never previously displayed the slightest interest. To her, it was just one more thing about me that needed fixing. She would remind me how harmful it can be to stare directly at the sun, although I never suffered any ill effects from doing so just long enough to generate a sneeze.

But then, only the other night, I saw a comedian on TV doing a bit about the funny ways different people sneeze. And sure enough, one of the types he made fun of was us "light-sneezers." So now I know there must be others around. It started me thinking about forming some kind of light-sneezers' society, to compare notes and see what else we might have in common. Who knows, maybe there's some correlation between light-sneezing and intelligence, or sexual preference, or propensity towards criminality.

Sneezing in itself is of course a most remarkable act. I have seen it compared (presumably for the enlightenment of those who have never experienced one or the other) with having an orgasm. A good sneeze certainly can provide a real sense of satisfaction. But why should *light* trigger it, and only in a certain select group of us? I don't know, and I'm not sure if anybody does. But finding out that I am not alone in this peculiarity has impelled me to tell you about another strange ability I have—which, as with the light-sneezing, others may share, but which I have so far never seen reported anywhere.

Although my hearing has always been quite good, I have, since childhood, been able, without moving, or doing anything that anybody can see, to "block out" any ordinary external sound, such as conversation, at will, and render myself unable to hear it. Thus, for example, if I am standing in line for a movie, and the people next to me have seen the film before, and are on the point of discussing the ending, which I don't want to know anything about, I have a way of "protecting" myself. I don't have to disturb the talkers, or do anything obvious like putting my fingers in my ears or moving farther away. I can just go on standing there, and yet not hear another word of what they are saying.

How do I do it? I start humming very softly to myself, and then I "click" something in my ears which somehow magnifies the internal sound of my humming, and makes it sound so loud inside my head that I can't hear anything else. I don't know what it is exactly that I do, but the ear-click is similar to that associated with sudden changes of altitude in an elevator or airplane.

I am proud of this talent, but its usefulness is extremely limited. It requires considerable effort and concentration, and it is unfortunately no answer to the problem of urban noise, to which I happen to be quite sensitive, since all it does, in effect, is to drown out one sound with another.

I have no idea whether ear-clicking and light-sneezing are in any way related. It may be that only a small proportion of light-sneezers can claim, like me, to be ear-clickers as well. But there is yet one more thing that I have been able to do since about the age of eight which I feel I must share with you, since it too surely sets me off from the vast majority of my fellow creatures.

Believe it or not, *I can say the alphabet backward just as fast as I can say it forward!* Just why I ever taught myself to do this I cannot remember. It was certainly not a school assignment. The idea might have been given me by a quiz-book I had which, I remember, contained the question, "In what occupation would it be useful to know the alphabet backwards?" The answer was, "Theater Usher." But I had no leanings in that direction, and have never "ushed" in my life. And no stranger or friend has ever approached me beseechingly with any urgent need to have the alphabet recited backwards for any other purpose.

Here again, therefore, I find myself endowed with a gift of questionable utility. But that doesn't necessarily make it any less of a blessing. As far as ordinary talents go, mine don't go very far. I can't play a musical instrument or speak a foreign language. I can't even ski or knit or ride a horse. My consolation, however, is that millions of people can do those things, while I may be the only light-sneezing ear-clicking alphabet-reverser in this whole neck of the woods.

Santa Barbara 1991

179

Prone Like a Stone

There are things you can only learn
Lying on the ground.
There are things you can only see
When your eyelids caress the grass.
There are things you cannot smell
Until your nostrils are filled with earth.
There are languages you cannot understand
Until you have been deafened by
    the thunder of a marching ant.

San Francisco 1967

A Flier's World

This is my world—wind, wings, and solitude,
This is my life, forever here to fly—
Each landing but an empty interlude,
Each flight a new homecoming to the sky.

San Jose, California, 1958

Flight of Fancy

One day when I was flying about in my little single-seater, I saw a man floating in the air, looking very relaxed. In one hand he held a string, which trailed down to the ground.

"What are you doing?" I called to him.

"I'm flying a kite," he replied.

"Where is the kite?"

"Down in my garden, on the other end of this string."

I started to laugh. "You silly man," I said, "don't you see the joke? You're not flying the kite—the *kite* is flying *you!*"

"*Spoilsport!*" he screamed, and at that instant began a precipitous descent.

Berkeley 1961

The Call of the Tame

We found a dead bird in our back garden one morning last week, somewhat mangled, and surrounded by a scattering of its feathers—evidently the victim of one of the savage feline night stalkers which in the daytime disguise themselves as our neighbors' lovable household pets. That day happened to be Thanksgiving, and I tried to make some feeble joke about our having got two Thanksgiving birds for the price of one. But we were both a little upset at coming so starkly upon a murder scene in the middle of our own little peaceful world.

Still fresh in my mind were that week's news pictures of murdered priests lying on some other lawn in a place called El Salvador. It seems that *killing*, for all the opposition it has received over the years from highly-respected sources, is still alive and well on this earth. Neither cats nor people have yet been persuaded to abandon the practice entirely.

About people, as we know them today, I have my hopes. Most human killing these days seems, at least as a nonofficial activity, to have become restricted to those whom we know collectively as criminals, crusaders, and crazies. Educational and medical advances (including compulsory brain surgery, which I am all in favor of, if it can have the desired results) may soon effectively control this problem.

But what are we to do about cats, and all the other living creatures (including the micro-organisms in our own bodies) to whom killing is a "natural" and usually essential

181

activity? What chance is there of re-educating the whole family of Nature so that no member kills any other member any more?

I do have an answer, but it is one whose details may take some time to work out. In a word, my answer is communication. As a rule, the better we communicate, the less desire or need we have to kill each other. The task, then, is to develop—or, more likely, to discover, for it may already actually exist (like the radio waves which were there for all those aeons before we were able to detect and use them)—a common language for all forms of life. I have already given it a name: NIMALANG—from "aNIMA-LANGuage" (since its development will no doubt first occur among the "higher" species which we call animals). I expect the discovery of Nimalang to be one of the most revolutionary events of all time. When cats and birds can truly communicate, the whole chain of predation will fall apart.

I realize that this vision sounds messianic. And I know I am not the first to dream that the lion will someday lie down with the lamb. But in this age of scientific miracles, it is surely not out of all bounds to conceive that this improvement of communication will be related to the development of some new nonbiological means of sustenance, perhaps derived directly from the sun, which will make possible an end to the entire system of life preying upon life.

In the meantime, I can only wish success to all those who are trying, in so many different ways, to make the world at least a slightly less savage place for all the creatures who live in it.

Santa Barbara 1989

Thinklings

I have to assume that (at least to some extent) you care what I think. Here, then, are some thoughts which have come to me at various times, which I hope you may find of interest:

❖ Why must TV documentaries, regardless of subject, nearly always have a musical background? I often find this very distracting.

❖ A definition of fame: When people don't cash your check because your signature is worth more than the amount of the check.

❖ I conceive the weird possibility that scientists may someday be able to create (purely for experimental purposes) miniature human beings about the size of rats, and with the same life-span as rats.

❖ The Ancient Egyptians worshipped three things for which I myself also have very high regard: Cats, the Sun, and the Scarab or Dung-Beetle. I particularly admire the Dung-Beetle because it doesn't have to kill anything else to remain alive, but takes as its sustenance what has already been rejected, and what we consider obnoxious. This also gives us a very practical benefit, in helping to keep down flies (which breed in the same material).

How to Change Things
By force and terror.
By economic and social pressure.
By love, friendship, and persuasion.
By changing yourself.

❖ Capital Punishment, besides being barbaric, is also a waste of potentially good experimental material. If we must retain such a penalty, let the condemned person be declared legally dead, and then placed in the hands of competent medical researchers.

❖ Terrorists might get much better results, and achieve much more social acceptance, if, instead of using violence, they employed *ridicule*. I envisage a nonviolent terrorist group known as the *Ridiculists* making use of this devastating weapon to secure their goals.

❖ Someday some human being will be selected as the first ever to have all the experiences of his or her life fully recorded from birth to death. Eventually more and more people's lives will be similarly recorded. Fast play-back techniques will be developed, enabling future generations to re-live entire lives, as we read a book.

❖ It seems remarkable that practically the whole of World War II was fought in black and white, and at 78 r.p.m.

❖ In the last thousand years, our society has seen a great change of emphasis from obligations to rights—a tendency which may now have gone too far. Is it not time, perhaps, for the Statue of Liberty to be joined by a Statue of Responsibility?

The Chief Points of My Religion
1. Love yourself.
2. Love whatever resembles you.
3. Seek resemblances everywhere, and in everything.

❖ Why are novels and short stories not usually illustrated any more, as they used to be? Whatever the reason, I regret the loss.

❖ Idea: a *Spending Society*. Members in attendance at any meeting each put up a given sum, say $5, and the purpose of the meeting is to decide how to spend the money, and then immediately do so.

❖ Now that even pro-gun groups have accepted screening at airports, based on the idea of passenger planes and the ground areas immediately around them being "no-gun territory," couldn't this idea be extended to broader and broader areas, until eventually the whole nation is a no-gun zone?

❖ I wonder how much longer it will be before a person in good health will voluntarily have a part of his or her body removed and replaced with an artificial part because the artificial part will in every way be superior and preferable.

❖ Among the ironies of modern life:
(1) People getting food hand-outs who are obviously over-weight and would benefit from fasting.
(2) More and more labor-saving devices, while people become sluggish and have to devise artificial exercises to keep fit.

❖ Women who succeed in politics or business often seem to do so by showing that they can be as tough and "manly" as men are supposed to be. When will we get a truly "motherly" leader?

❖ How long will it be before we have some means of recording our dreams while we sleep, and playing them back later when we are awake?

❖ There ought to be *Investigative Personal Counsellors,* who don't just have you come and sit in their office, but who make house-calls and study your daily life, home and work circum-stances, etc.

❖ An original riddle: You can take mine and I can take yours. But even if you take mine, I still have it. And when you take it, you may find that I didn't even have one. What is it?
Answer: My temperature.

❖ *On Rights:* A distinction ought to be drawn between what are considered "fundamental human rights" (which I personally don't believe in) and what we might call "reasonable human expectations" (which I find much easier to accept).

❖ Sometimes people have to overcome their own names. Wouldn't it have seemed terrible to go through life with a name like Noel *Coward!*—and yet, when we hear the name, we don't even think about its meaning.

❖ One of the most moving passages I have ever read occurs in Victor Frankl's book, *Death Camp to Existentialism.* He recalls that one night in the Nazi death camp, the man in the next bunk was having a bad dream, tossing and moaning. Frankl's impulse was to take pity and wake him, but as he reached out to do so, he suddenly realized that no dream, however bad, could be as bad as the reality this man would be returning to when he woke.

❖ It seems oddly appropriate that brakes and tires should *scream* in the very same kind of situations when any person involved would also be most likely to scream.

❖ Isn't it ironic that, in a country whose whole economy is based on credit, our most popular prayer should include the plea to "forgive us our debts as we forgive our debtors"?

❖ The desolate central region of Australia is known as its "Dead Heart." I myself almost always get depressed around Christmas, and think of it as the "Dead Heart of the Year."

❖ I would like to see the inauguration of a service which would enable invalids to enjoy "hiking" to places reachable only on foot, being carried along the trails by strong bearers.

❖ Patrick Henry is most famous for declaring, "Give me liberty or give me death!" in 1775. His very last words, uttered on his deathbed many years later in 1799, had no connection with that remark, and yet they strangely echo it. What he said was: "It will give relief, or prove fatal immediately?"

❖ One great social boon apparently not yet invented by science would be an effective drug, method, or device for the safe temporary elimination of the sex drive. An amazing number of our current social problems could thereby be much more easily controlled.

❖ The chief function of government should be providing people with what they most want and need: better lives through better bodies and better brains. In particular, brain research should be a top government priority.

❖ Where is it written that shoes, socks, gloves, etc. must match?

❖ Among the most wonderful things I know of:
   Radio
   Dreams
   Healing
   Memory
   The loyalty of a dog

Exile

(The following was written in Orange, California, on May 30, 1966.

It shows strong influence of the "Beat" poets.

My friends were in the San Francisco Bay Area and Los Angeles, while I was "exiled" in Orange, between voyages on the "Floating University.")

I am sick with longing for crazy friends—
Friends you can drop in on at three o'clock in the morning who fill their apartments with junk, and you have to literally climb in over it
Friends who send their wives out to work in bars, while they sit at home reading Philosophy, and taking clocks impossibly apart
Friends who sell up everything, and take three-year trips around the world to prove what you can do with a crippled hip
Friends who fight their wars by getting someone to ring your bell and throw a pie at you
Friends who never marry their fat wives, but start children's day-nurseries with them, stocked with nineteen varieties of noisemakers
Friends who eat fried chicken three times a day for four years, and engage in endless litigation over fraudulent freezers and spoiled specimens
Friends who throw pots and ride unicycles and shop only at the Goodwill and major in extracurricular activities and stare vacantly out of the window all day and collect empty milk cartons—and appear to be actually alive
I am sick with longing for friends with whom I used to exchange dear sweet lessons in insanity.

Only 13 years before men reached the Moon, the highest mountain on Earth was finally climbed for the first time. This was of course celebrated as a glorious event (I remember how it was announced on the same day as the Coronation of Queen Elizabeth II); but to me, at the age of 19, what it meant was one less world left to conquer.

Everest Defiled

The Goddess of Endeavor lies aravished,
And virgin snows befouled in honor's name;
Last of terrestrial glories lost forever,
Everest, I am humbled in thy shame.

In darkness now enshrouded lie thy bastions,
Forlorn thy frozen pinnacles look down,
Eternity, her sanctuary broken,
Broods upon thy desecrated crown.

Yet if forbidden beauty's violation
Must to the record add of human crime,
If Earth's most cherished citadel must crumble,
Why could not that conquest have been mine?

London 1953

The Great
Race Space

I hold these truths to be self-evident: that all people are not created equal; and that, even in a paradise like my own city of Santa Barbara, the amount of melanin in your complexion, and the language spoken by your ancestors, can have a more than chance relationship to the type of work you do and the part of town you live in.

A person would have to be pretty blind not to notice, for example, that in our community most of the menial work on the roads, in the parks and gardens, in the hotels and restaurants—the work that would have been allotted to slaves if slavery were still officially in existence, is performed by people who speak to each other in Spanish rather than English, and who appear to be at least culturally related to the Mexicans from whom political control of this area was taken by force some 140 years ago. Were it not un-Santa Barbaran to utter such a thought, this might be called a classic example of a subjugated race turned by the harsh realities of conquest into a permanently servile class.

Of course, they themselves had done the same thing to the Indians only a few years earlier, but the Indians, for better or worse, responded to this indignity by dying out in large numbers, thus saving themselves from a similar fate. In any case, it's hard to look at any of these developments in terms of historical justice. If we say we ought to give California back to Mexico, shouldn't Mexico then be given back to Spain? Then, depending on how far you want to take this, we must allow that Spain should be given back to the Moors, and Morocco to the Roman Empire.

The fact remains that ethnic determinism is alive and well in Santa Barbara, which I suppose is O.K., so long as you don't call it racism. Our citizens of African descent tend, for whatever reason, to concentrate in a very clearly-defined, comparatively low-rent district (not, for Heaven's sake, to be confused with a "ghetto"). In contrast, my own Jewish minority (for whose communities in Europe the word "ghetto" was originally invented) is comparatively well-dispersed, but is so accustomed to persecution that even here it almost intentionally maintains a cautiously low profile. A recent public Jewish Festival in a neighborhood park was, to my knowledge, the first of its kind. Most non-Jewish residents of Santa Barbara probably don't even know where its large synagogue is located.

Those of our residents whose background lies in the Far East (which, from the perspective of California, really ought to be called the Near West) also seem to be still struggling to overcome ancient prejudices, and have yet even to try for a seat on our City Council. The last Oriental who had anything to do with shaking up Santa Barbara (we won't count the nonresident Japanese submarine commander who shelled a nearby coastal oil installation in 1942) appears to have been Gin Chow, a Chinese who died in 1934, and who, according to at least two local historians, is supposed to have predicted the big 1925 earthquake two years, to the day, in advance. (I don't believe this, but it's a pretty story.)

Despite our cherished ideals and constitutional guarantees, this whole subject of racial and cultural differences and how we handle them is still so sensitive that I feel obliged to insert here a "disclaimer," assuring you (whether I really mean it or not) that my intention is not to offend anybody or to stir up any kind of trouble. But I also reserve the right to state the obvious, which is that, even if we really want to do so, we still have some distance to go in filling those gaps between our various ethnic groups which one might call the Great Race Space.

Santa Barbara 1989

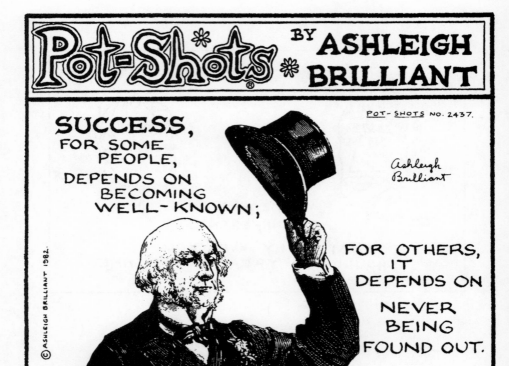

Pot-Shots BY ASHLEIGH BRILLIANT

POT-SHOTS NO. 2437.

Ashleigh Brilliant

© ASHLEIGH BRILLIANT 1982.

SUCCESS, FOR SOME PEOPLE, DEPENDS ON BECOMING WELL-KNOWN;

FOR OTHERS, IT DEPENDS ON NEVER BEING FOUND OUT.

Disgrace:
from White House
to Our House

Political events do not often set my pen wagging, but a good national scandal is hard to resist. In this country, we were presented with two major ones within a dozen years, as commemorated in the following epic. It was written when the hunt was in full cry to incriminate President Ronald Reagan in the so-called Iran-Contra Affair, with a search for evidence such as had been the downfall of his predecessor in the debacle called Watergate:

A Visit from Saint Nix

'Twas the night before Christmas, but there in the White House
Our leader sat lonely, as if in a lighthouse;
The stockings were hanging, but since he felt nervous,
The chimneys were guarded by brave Secret Service;
Nancy already was snug in her bed,
Where visions of fashion-shows danced in her head;
"But what meaning has Christmas," the President ponders,
"If I can't turn my mind from Iran and the Contras?
How, if North and Poindexter just won't take the rap,
Can I settle my brains for a long winter's nap?"
Then out on the lawn there arose such a clatter,
He sprang from his chair to see what was the matter.
And what to his wondering eyes should appear,
But a big helicopter, from which loud and clear
A voice boomed in greeting, "Hello there, how's tricks, Ron!"
He knew in a moment it must be Saint Nixon!

193

He was dressed as of old from his head to his foot
In a dark, "sincere" tie, and a blue business suit,
And his friends were all with him, of Watergate fame,
And he whistled and shouted, and called them by name:
"Now, Liddy! now, Mitchell! now, Ehrlichman, John!
On, E. Howard Hunt! on, H. L. Haldeman!"
And then, in a twinkling, he somehow contrived
To jimmy the window, and climb up inside.
"Well, Ronald my boy," chortled jolly Saint Nix,
"You've got yourself into a hell of a fix!"
A big empty sack he had flung on his back,
And he looked like a burglar, about to ransack.
He said not a word more, but went straight to his job,
And, leaving no prints upon any door-knob,
He crept past all the White House's dark sleeping shapes,
Looking for files, and especially for tapes;
And, whatever might help Ronald's critics attack,
He quickly removed, and dropped into his sack.
The President watched as he searched every shelf,
And chuckled with pleasure in spite of himself.
A wink and a nod from this jolly old friend
Made him see that his troubles were now at an end.
Then, making his sign of crossed fingers unseen,
Saint Nixon returned to his waiting machine,
To his sack gave a heave, though its burden of guilt
Was so heavy by now that it just about spilt;
But Ron heard him call 'mid the whirling blades' lift:
"It's not what I leave—what I take is my gift!"
And he heard him exclaim at the copter's last sighting:
"Never say it on tape! Never put it in writing!"

Santa Barbara, December 24, 1986

Half a year later, the Iran-Contra investigation was appearing on national TV, with a prolonged series of Congressional hearings centering on one of the key figures, Colonel Oliver North. As reported in the following letter, published in the Santa Barbara News-Press, this outrageous affair thus even came to involve a very special member of our own household, to whose memory this book is dedicated:

Cat-astrophe

Since everybody else in the country seems to have vehement feelings, one way or another, about Oliver North and the Iran-Contra hearings, you may like to know that our cat Gaga recently expressed a very strong opinion of his own.

On the first day of Col. North's testimony, we left one TV set on all the time, even when nobody was in the room. It was the set upon which Gaga has long been in the habit of reclining, usually without any noticeable interest in whatever program might happen to be on.

On this occasion, however (and it will necessarily linger in our memory), we came into the room to find the TV no longer working, an unmistakable odor emanating from it, and various other evidence, of a liquid nature, to indicate that Gaga, at some point in the session, had felt so moved by what he heard that he relieved his feelings directly down into the TV through the ventilation-slots on top, causing a short-circuit.

Gaga had already fled the scene (we found him "innocently" asleep in another room) and, since nobody else had been present, we will never know exactly what remark from Col. North, or from some member of the House-Senate Committee, triggered from our normally very well-behaved cat this eloquent comment on the whole proceedings.

Santa Barbara, July 11, 1987

Pot-Shots BY ASHLEIGH BRILLIANT

POT-SHOTS NO. 3326.

ISN'T IT WONDERFUL!

INSIDE EVERY
LITTLE BEAM
OF LIGHT,

A RAINBOW
IS SLEEPING.

© ASHLEIGH BRILLIANT 1985

Ashleigh Brilliant

Local Color

First came the rain, then the sun, then the rainbow. There it was, stretching across the sky above our protecting hills, that lovely arc of color which, no matter how many times you see it, and no matter how well you know the scientific explanation, still somehow seems miraculous. But I was in a hurry, and my walk was taking me in the opposite direction. The only way I could keep enjoying that spectacular vision was by pausing every now and then and turning around.

But it made me feel guilty to treat a miracle so casually, and each time I turned around, I feared it would already be gone. I kept thinking of those lines from a poem we learned at school:

What is this life, if, full of care,
We have no time to stand and stare?

I felt even worse when somebody walking in the other direction, a young woman whom I didn't even know, actually said to me as we passed, "Have you seen the rainbow!" and I had to assure her that I had seen it, and then (partly out of politeness) pause and admire it with her.

What is it about rainbows that makes people want to share them? As I hurried on, my mind raced through its little catalog of rainbow lore. I thought about the legend of the crock of gold, and about Judy Garland's wonderful land "somewhere over the rainbow," and that other old song about the poor fellow who's "always chasing rainbows"

197

and who cries that "my dreams are just like all my schemes—ending in the sky." Many people apparently see the rainbow as something essentially unreal, which I suppose is a feeling we get because it doesn't last, but comes and goes mysteriously.

But (it occurred to me) there's another idea about the rainbow also prevailing in our culture, which goes back at least as far as the story of Noah and the Ark, and which sees the rainbow as a symbol of *hope*. Of course this must derive from the fact that rainbows tend to appear when the rain is ending and the sun is coming out. The Bible turns that into a "sign" of the benevolence of God, a promise that he will never again seek to destroy all life on Earth, as he supposedly came close to doing with the Great Flood. I have always liked that story, but Noah was no Dr. Dolittle, and I would have liked it even more had he not, as soon as the Flood was over, felt obliged to start killing and sacrificing some of the very animals he had helped to save. (Children are not usually told that part of the story.)

Does the rainbow, then, mean hope, or does it mean illusion? Or does it mean that hope and illusion are ultimately the same thing? Fortunately those are not the only possibilities. In some cultures the rainbow is seen as a kind of *bridge* between the worlds of gods and men—an idea which I personally find very appealing. If we must live all our days in doubt about the true nature of the universe, aren't we lucky to have, at least occasionally, this beautiful suggestion of a cosmic link between what we know, and all that we can never know.

With this happy insight, I reached my destination—my house on Valerio Street—and dashed up the steps, realizing only then just why I had been in such a hurry. "Quick!" I shouted in from the doorway to my wife, "Come out and see the rainbow, before it fades!" She rushed out to join me, and there on our front path, holding each other close, we both just stood and stared.

Santa Barbara 1990

Open End

If all's well that ends well, I would naturally like this book to end well. But how should a book like this end? I can't come on like Porky Pig and stammer, "That's All, Folks!" because that isn't really all at all. There's much more where all this came from, i.e. in my head and in my files. And I would like nothing better than to be able to go on indefinitely sharing ideas, feelings, and experiences with you. So please let me know what you liked or didn't like in here, and whether you really want more of this kind of thing.

A catalogue of all my works, including the Pot-Shots® books, cards, and other products for which I am (at least so far) best known, is also available. The current (1992) price for a catalogue and set of samples is U.S. $2. Please enclose that amount, or its equivalent in your own time and currency.

My address is:

Ashleigh Brilliant
117 W. Valerio St.
Santa Barbara
California 93101 U.S.A.

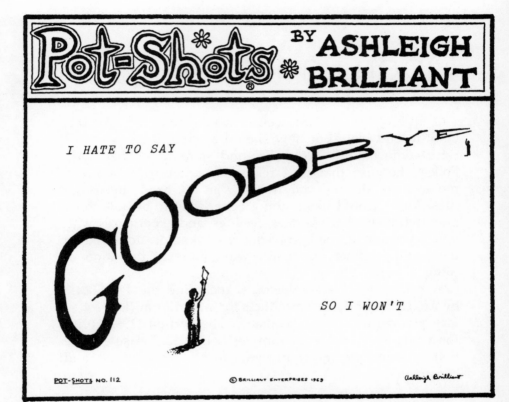

Other Books by Ashleigh Brilliant

The Pot-Shots® Series—Books of Brilliant Thoughts®

I. I May Not Be Totally Perfect, but Parts of Me Are Excellent. *Hard cover: 0-912800-66-6, $12.95; Soft cover: 0-912800-67-4, $7.95.*

II. I Have Abandoned My Search for Truth, and Am Now Looking for a Good Fantasy. *Hard cover: 0-912800-97-6, $12.95; Soft cover: 0-912800-94-1, $7.95.*

III. Appreciate Me Now and Avoid the Rush. *Hard cover: 0-912800-89-5, $12.95; Soft cover, 0-912800-90-9, $7.95.*

IV. I Feel Much Better, Now that I've Given Up Hope. *Hard cover, 0-88007-145-1, $12.95; Soft cover, 0-88007-147-8, $7.95.*

V. All I Want Is a Warm Bed and a Kind Word and Unlimited Power. *Hard cover, 0-88007-155-9, $12.95; Soft cover, 0-88007-156-7, $7.95.*

VI. I Try to Take One Day at a Time, but Sometimes Several Days Attack Me at Once. *Hard cover, 0-88007-161-3, $12.95; Soft cover, 0-88007-162-1, $7.95.*

VII. We've Been Through So Much Together, and Most of It Was Your Fault. *Hard cover, 0-88007-182-6, $12.95; Soft cover, 0-88007-183-4, $7.95.*

The Great Car Craze: *How Southern California Collided with the Automobile in the 1920's*

Dr. Brilliant discusses the human, technological, aesthetic, and ecological effects as the country frantically embraced mobility as one of life's highest values. *Hard cover, 0-88007-172-9, $19.95.*

Woodbridge Press, Santa Barbara, California 93160

Prices subject to change.